WORKING
WITH
GEMSTONES

BOOKS BY THE SAME AUTHOR

Gemstones of the British Isles
The Crust of the Earth
Arran with Camera and Sketchbook
In the Hills of Breadalbane
The Cairngorms on Foot and Ski
On Foot in the Cairngorms
On Ski in the Cairngorms
Ski Track on the Battlefield
The Tatra Mountains
Our Neighbour Worlds
Strange World of the Moon
Moon Atlas
Surface of the Moon
The Moon
Exploring the Planets
Facing the Universe
The Interior Planets
The World of Mars
The Old Moon and the New
Life Beyond the Earth
Life, Mind and Galaxies
Life Unlimited (in preparation)
The Unity of Europe

WORKING
WITH
GEMSTONES

V. A. Firsoff

DAVID & CHARLES: NEWTON ABBOT

736·2028

FIR

0 7153 6188 0

Set in 11 on 13 point Joanna
and printed in Great Britain by
Redwood Burn Limited
Trowbridge & Esher
for David & Charles (Holdings) Limited
South Devon House Newton Abbot Devon

CONTENTS

ILLUSTRATIONS

ILLUSTRATIONS

ACKNOWLEDGEMENTS

THIS BOOK HAS BEEN WRITTEN IN COLLABORATION WITH HERBERT Scarfe, who has acted as technical adviser. He has also provided a series of photographs illustrating working sequences and Figs. 19–24, 26, 28 and 32–4. (Other drawings, save on p. 150 and Figs. 1, 36 and 37 are my own.) His valuable help is greatly appreciated. The text, however, is mine, and the opinions expressed are entirely my own.

I am further indebted to Ken Attwood for kindly supplying a photograph and particulars of his home-built combination unit; to Chapman & Hall for permission to quote from G. F. Smith's *Gemstones*; to A. H. & W. A. Reed for allowing me to include the drawing and description of the tyre tumbler from Lyn and Ray Cooper's book *New Zealand Gemstones*; and to the following firms, which have placed at my disposal photographs, drawings and/or other material relating to the machines, tools and accessories produced and/or marketed by them: Ammonite Ltd, of Llandow Industrial Estate, Cowbridge, Glamorgan, Wales; M. L. Beach (Products) Ltd, 41 Church Street, Twickenham, Middlesex; Dorothy Blake Custom Jewelry, 1700 South Bedford Street, Los Angeles, California 90035; Gemrocks Ltd, Halton House, 20–3 Holborn, London EC1; Lapidary Wholesale Supply Co, 46 Walmsley Street, Hull HU3 1QD; PMR Lapidary Equipment & Supplies, Smithy House, Atholl Road, Pitlochry, Perthshire; Wessex Impex Ltd, Gemini, Lanham Lane, Winchester, Hampshire; and Whithear Lapidary Co, of Ballards Lane, London N3 1XL.

Their help, too, has been of material assistance in completing my work, but it will be understood that the selection of machinery illustrated and described in it, while representative, is to some extent arbitrary and implies no criticism or censure of the many equivalent and excellent products that it has been impossible to consider for reasons of space.

V. A. F.

1

THE RAW
MATERIALS OF THE ART

INTRODUCTION

THE LAPIDARY'S ART CONSISTS IN FASHIONING RAW PIECES OF ROCK OR
stone into decorative objects, such as cut and polished gems to be
mounted in jewellery, or small articles intended as mantelpiece or
table ornaments, in which his work shades into that of a sculptor.
Engraved gems are miniature sculptures, requiring a high degree of
artistic skill, as well as technical perfection, a marriage of technology
and creative imagination.

   This book is addressed primarily to the amateur lapidarist. But the
difference between amateur and professional is one of degree only,
and the point that the latter draws his livelihood from cutting
stones is largely adventitious. However a professional not only can,
but must, devote more time to it and may afford better and more
expensive equipment which has to be used skilfully and economically to make it worth-while. An amateur may be anything, from an
occasional weekend dabbler to an enthusiastic owner of a well-
equipped workshop—a professional in all but name. All trades and
professions have their mystiques and mumbo-jumbos, whose main
object is to impress, confuse and discourage the uninitiated in the
collective interests of the trade. This an aspiring hobbyist need not
take too seriously. His pursuit is made much easier by the existence
of lapidary clubs in most major centres of population, which largely
eliminate the necessity of acquiring, maintaining and housing
expensive machinery. On the other hand, those with a mechanical
bend of mind may enjoy pitting their ingenuity against the problem

of constructing their own machines. Nowadays the lapidary craft is taught in many schools and technical colleges. Clubs, too, usually provide some tuition for the beginners. Yet, while it is true that manual skill cannot be acquired by reading books, a few timely hints can save many tears, and sound theoretical knowledge shortens the road of personal exploration.

In the pages that follow an attempt is made to cater for the needs of all these classes of person within a modest compass and at a price readily accessible to an average pocket.

We shall see later on that there exist simple methods of working with gemstones, requiring a minimum of equipment and skill, and dispensing with power drive at the cost of some 'elbow-grease'. Thus one need not be a 'compleat lapidary' to extract some fun and profit from this fascinating hobby, which is distinctly 'moreish'. The casual finder of a diamond, ruby or emerald will be well advised to entrust its cutting to an experienced firm of good repute. Such firms, however, are not very keen on cutting semi-precious stones and may decline to do so outright. This is quite apart from the cost, which may be disproportionately high in relation to the value of the finished product. There are, of course, less classy establishments which specialise in this type of work at reasonable prices. The situation, however, is not without its pitfalls.

In G. F. Herbert Smith's book *Gemstones* (1952 edn), p 351, the author recommends that:

A note of caution should be sounded for the benefit of those who, while on holiday by the sea, may pick up a pretty pebble or two and may think how nice it would be to have them cut to wear as ornaments. It is possible to find suitable material, clear and transparent, though possibly water-worn, and either colourless or of an attractive tint, but such material is far less common and is hardly likely to reward a casual search. If the stones be taken to a local lapidary, it has been known to happen that, lest he lose business by explaining that they are not worth cutting ... he accepts the job, but substitutes other stones, already cut, bought by the gross, or even paste (jeweller's glass); the customer, on the other hand, receives a pretty bawble, and is seldom grateful if he be told that he might have got one like it for a fraction of the price he paid.

I have known customers who were even less grateful, for they professed to have had inferior stones substituted for their finds, or accused the lapidary of having returned only a small fraction of the original material. A reputable firm is unlikely to do that, and because a lion's share of the rough material may be inevitably lost in the cutting, these accusations are probably ill-founded in most cases. Still, to rid himself of such suspicions, a weekend or holiday gem-hunter may do well to try his hand at doing the job himself.

Lapidary work as a craft or hobby may be usefully combined with gem-hunting, or 'fossicking', as this is called in Australia, which requires some mineralogical and geological knowledge. This can be found in specialised works. Alternatively material suitable for all grades of workmanship can be purchased at assorted prices from dealers, who regularly advertise in appropriate journals, such as Gems in Great Britain or Lapidary Journal in the USA, and many of whom are listed on pp 193–202.

Yet even those who do not intend to engage in any prospecting of their own cannot do without some basic mineralogical information, for raw material cannot be successfully worked unless its properties are understood.

ROCKS AND MINERALS

A stone may be a rock or a mineral, the difference being that a mineral is homogeneous, consisting of the same chemical substance throughout. A rock need not be homogeneous, and is more often than not a mixture of various minerals. A large amount of a mineral may make a boulder, a rock or even a mountain. For example, marble, which is indurated limestone, hardened by volcanic or magmatic (magma is molten rock which need not originate in a volcano) heat, is a more or less pure carbonate of lime and therefore mineral, but does occur in large masses. Serpentinite, or crude serpentine, sometimes found in association with marble, or produced by the chemical weathering of ultrabasic igneous rocks (see below), is similarly a rock, although it may also be classed as a mineral. Obsidian, a glassy variety of acid lava, suitable for lapidary purposes, is a rock of the same chemical composition as granite, but its ingredients are so intimately fused that it again deserves to be considered a mineral. The same applies to mineral coal, which in the black variety of lignite known under the name of jet has been used for jewellery.

Typically, however, rocks are mineral puddings, which is crudely obvious in *conglomerate*, even referred to as puddingstone and made up of rounded pebbles cemented together by a limestone, sandstone or similar matrix. A comparable rock consisting of angular fragments is called *breccia* (brecha), and when of volcanic origin—*agglomerate*. Granite is the commonest example of crystalline igneous (fire-wrought) rock, composed mainly of intergrown crystals of felspar, quartz and mica, but sometimes containing small proportions of such gem minerals as topaz, beryl, spinel, corundum, zircon, sphene, almandine garnet, tourmaline, and fluorspar.

Most rocks provide building or sculpting rather than lapidary material, but some, in addition to those already mentioned, are sufficiently hard and durable, as well as attractive to be used for small ornaments, beads and the like. Some small-grained porphyries, which are of the same chemical make-up as granite, but consist of an undifferentiated, or a finely crystalline ground-mass in which large crystals of felspar or quartz are scattered singly giving the rock a pleasing speckled appearance, may qualify for this purpose. Jade, beloved by the Chinese and ancient Mexican craftsmen, is well-known as an ornamental stone of volcanic origin.

The suitability of a rock for lapidary purposes depends, apart from attractive appearance, upon at least approximately homogeneous hardness, without which it tends to disintegrate and does not readily take a uniform polish. Conglomerates of small pebbles, which may include agate, carnelian, jasper, etc, require induration by magmatic heat. This gives them a more coherent texture, as well as adding colour and translucency to the otherwise dull quartz balls, which account for most of their pebble content, so that they make good-looking polished sections. But even softer stones such as alabaster, are eligible for ornamental objects, though not for beads, as they would suffer excessive wear.

There are three main classes of rocks: *igneous*, which have con-solidated from molten condition; *sedimentary*, formed by the deposi-tion, or sedimentation, of the products of decay of other rocks (pebbles and gravels, grit, sand, clay, mud or silt) and/or of organic matter (sea-shells, skeletons of marine animals, dead vegetation), and eventually cemented into hard compact mass by pressure and chemical binding; and *metamorphic*, obtained from sedimentary rocks by alteration, or metamorphosis, due to heat and pressure with the attendant induration (as in fired clay) and partial crystallisation of the ingredients. This type of rock when exposed to the great shearing stresses arising from the creep and folding of the earth's crust, often acquires a foliated (leafy) structure and is then known as *schist*. Chemical changes due to permeation by hot corrosive fluids, described by the term of pneumatolysis, may affect both sedimentary and igneous formations and are a frequent source of gemstones and industrial minerals. Total crystallisation of a sedimentary rock will give it igneous structure, as exemplified in *gneiss* (nice), which is a kind of layered granite, whose main constituents (felspar, quartz and mica) have been segregated into layers, Swiss-roll fashion. Gneiss, however, may also be formed by the application of shearing stress to granite; and granites may themselves have begun their existence as sediments. Rocks are also subject to chemical weathering, and, as already indicated, ultrabasic formations thus decay to serpentinite, since they contain a high proportion of olivine which is altered to serpentine.

Igneous rocks are subdivided into *plutonic* or *intrusive* and *volcanic* or *extrusive*. In the case of the first the molten material (magma) has risen from the bowels of the earth through the cracks and weaknesses in the upper strata, without reaching the surface, and has set hard comparatively slowly under the weight of the overlying rocks. The resulting structure is crystalline, and the deeper underground the intrusion lay and the more massive it was, the more slowly will it have cooled, giving rise to correspondingly larger crystals. The extrusive volcanics have consolidated from lava on the surface under atmospheric pressure or have been ejected from the volcano as gas-imbued loose 'ash' and pebbles (lapilli), which in due course consolidate into hard grey rock called tuff. All lavas contain gas cavities, and it is in these that chalcedony, agate and zeolites are deposited from hot solutions in the course of cooling. A gas-rich lava boils and bubbles as it cools rapidly in air and acquires a spongy structure, as in pumice, which is so light that it floats on water. Pumice is not much use to a lapidary, but slow-cooled volcanics may contain various gemstones, including diamond.

The igneous rocks are further divided horizontally into clans according to chemical composition, indicated by the proportion of silica, or silicon dioxide (SiO_2), which may be present in the pure form of quartz or bound in silicates (felspar, mica, augite, etc); and vertically according to the size of crystal-grain which is governed by the rate of cooling.

In the *acid clan*, where silica accounts for 65 per cent or more of the total weight and quartz is abundant, granite is the deep-seated, coarse-grained acid rock. The grain may vary from millimetre to centimetre size, but in giant granite, or granite pegmatite, it may exceed 4in (10cm). Aplite is a fine-grained, light-coloured variety. In porphyry, as we may recall, large crystals are scattered through a microcrystalline matrix. In rhyolite the matrix is glassy and the quartz grains are rounded, like currants, and, finally, obsidian is all glass and contains no crystals at all.

The other clans have similar divisions. The intermediate clan which ranges at between 65 and 55 per cent of silica, contains little or no quartz, and the sequence is: diorite, micro-diorite, diorite-porphyry, andesite. In the *basic clan* of gabbro, micro-gabbro and basalt the silica content drops below 55 per cent, quartz is usually absent and the orthoclase felspar, typical of the acid rocks, is largely replaced by plagioclase. The heavy ferromagnesian or mafic minerals, such as augite, hornblende, olivine, ilmenite, give these rocks a dark hue, which is often bluish or greenish. These features become intensified in the rare *ultrabasic* (*ultramafic*) rocks, exemplified by dunite and peridotite, which originate at great depths. Their silica content lies below 45 per cent, and felspar crystals disappear. Diamond is one of the accessory minerals of such low-silica rocks. The more basic a rock is, the darker and the heavier it will be.

All clans have their large-grain pegmatites and small-grain aplites, which occur in veins and larger masses, intruded at early and late stages of cooling respectively. The hot pegmatite magma carries a lot of gas, so that pegmatites usually contain large cavities, or *druses* (see plate, p 59), lined with crystals of the constituent minerals, which can grow unobstructed and may attain considerable size. The pegmatites are often characterised by high concentrations of rare minerals, and are a rich source of crystalline gemstones.

Good crystals may occasionally form in the solid rock as well, and, unless isolated by decay, have to be cut out of it. This is generally the case in metamorphic rocks, where crystallisation has been induced by heat and pressure. If the enveloping matrix is relatively soft, eg limestone or mica, the crystals can be dug out comparatively easily. Limestone can be dissolved out with acetic acid. This technique is also effective with most sandstones, whose grains are cemented with lime. But a compact igneous ground-mass is not so easy to deal with, and simply breaking or slicing it will not do either for there may be further good crystals inside it.

Well-formed (euhedral) crystals are generally harder and more resistant to erosion and chemical corrosion than the surrounding rock, so that they remain intact when the latter has decayed, weather out of it and become concentrated in river and beach gravels. The same is true of cavity fillings, such as agates and potato-stones, which look like potatoes and enclose crystal-lined cavities, or *geodes*. In particular the river gravels of Burma, Ceylon and the Transvaal are famed for a great variety of precious and semi-precious stones.

Conglomerates cemented from such beach or river material will inherit their gems, and these may in turn weather out of them. Something, however, is lost with each successive step. On the other hand, flawed specimens are the first to succumb to the wear, so that the water-worn stones are among the best. Unaltered sedimentary formations (sandstone, limestone, shale) are generally innocent of gems, but hot fluids emanating from magmatic intrusions and percolating through the cracks may generate mineral and crystal veins, such as the amethyst ones in some Irish sandstones.

Most of the valuable gem materials, however, come from mines, either worked expressly for this purpose as at the famous Minas Geraes in Brazil and the diamond pits of Kimberley in South Africa, or from mines concentrating on industrial minerals, where gemstones are merely a by-product of the operations. In this case the cheaper varieties of gemstone, such as agates or coloured quartzes, may be supplied by the hundredweight.

MINERALS AND GEMSTONES

As stated earlier, a mineral is a chemical substance of at least approximately constant composition, though it often contains minor impurities to which most of the varied colorations are due. In some complex minerals, such as garnets or felspars, the variation is continuous, so that different species shade into one another imperceptibly.

Minerals may be *amorphous* (which is the Greek for shapeless), or *massive*, or *crystalline* with the same composition, which depends on their mode of formation (see plate, p 59). The term massive is somewhat ambiguous, inasmuch as it may be applied to a jumble of poorly developed crystals, to crypto-crystalline stones where the crystals are too small to be distinguishable with the naked eye, or to structureless glass, as exemplified by obsidian. Glass results from rapid cooling from a melt, but may also be formed by the gelling of a dense solution; indeed, most massive material is deposited from solution, of which chalcedony—a massive form of silica—

and opal are useful examples. Agate is layered chalcedony, its onion-peel layers often differing not only in colour, but also in hardness which may have to be taken into account in cutting and polishing. The stone may split along the laminae if overheated or rapidly cooled. The softer layers abrade faster than the harder ones, which results in undercutting and a ribbed effect if too much pressure is applied. Glassy material inclines to be brittle and to splinter into nasty sharp sherds, which may require careful handling, for instance, in preparing a charge for the tumbling drum. Stones made up of closely packed crystals need special care in sawing, etc.

Massive material deposited from solution often has minute pores and is highly absorbent. Use is made of this property in the chemical staining of agates and the manufacture of Swiss lapis, which is red jasper imbued with Prussian blue. But by the same token such stones also absorb the lubricant used in sawing, which may result in ugly discoloration if oil or paraffin is used for lubrication. Turquoise and some opals are particularly sensitive and should be lubricated with water.

Thus the distinctions between minerals are not just a matter of theory; they have practical consequences of which a skilled lapidary must take heed. Indeed, he ought to be enough of a gemmologist to be able to identify his stones and rocks. This, however, is a vast subject far exceeding the scope of the present book, where it must be reduced to barest rudiments. Fuller information will be found in specialised works, which range from many-tomed compendia to short 'identifiers'.

To qualify as a gemstone, a mineral must be of attractive appearance when dressed, take good polish, and be sufficiently durable to resist wear. The latter requirement will vary with the use for which the stone is intended. Only very hard stones are suitable for rings. Softer varieties will do for pendants, necklaces or earrings, and quite soft stones, such as alabaster, lend themselves to carving and fashioning into standing ornaments. A gem is also expected to be rare and valuable, but this is a matter of supply and demand, which is to some extent governed by fashion, and has nothing to do with the intrinsic properties of the mineral itself. The most expensive gemstones: emerald, diamond, ruby and sapphire, are definitely precious; all others are usually described as semi-precious, and ornamental stones used for larger trinkets make the bottom grade. But we also have 'precious opal', 'precious garnet', 'precious serpentine', etc, which do not fit into this classification, such names being used mainly to distinguish them from the less valuable varieties of the comparable mineral.

Generally speaking trade names are highly confusing. For instance, 'oriental amethyst' is a violet variety of sapphire, and so a corundum, which is an aluminium oxide (Al_2O_3), whereas the true amethyst is a variety of quartz (SiO_2), owing its colour to a colloidal dispersion of iron; 'occidental topaz' is no topaz, which is properly a fluorosilicate of aluminium, but cairngorm or citrine and so a brown or yellow quartz; an 'oriental topaz' is a yellow sapphire; a 'Matura diamond' has nothing in common with real diamond, which is a transparent crystalline form of the element carbon and chemically identical with soot, for it is a colourless silicate of the metal zirconium; 'Bristol diamonds', 'Isle of Wight diamonds', 'Buxton diamonds' and other locally qualified diamonds, are all rock crystal, ie relatively cheap glass-clear quartz.

The attractiveness of a gemstone may reside in its colour or design, transparency and sparkle, known as fire, a special shimmer, described as chatoyancy or schiller, the rainbow play of reflected light, as in precious opal and labradorite, or some combination of these attributes. At times the beauty is asleep and does not come to light until awakened by the lapidary. Labradorite, an iridescent variety of felspar, will not reveal its butterfly-wing shimmer unless cut at an appropriate angle. Haematite, which is an oxide of iron (Fe_2O_3), looks anything but beautiful in the raw, but polishes to an untarnishable likeness of stainless steel, and is used for setting in such articles as signet rings or cuff-links.

The most valuable gems, however, are hard, transparent crystals, coloured or not, and possessed of fire, a property which will be considered more fully in Chapter 3. Massive gemstones may be transparent, but are more often translucent or opaque, as exemplified by turquoise, lapis lazuli or jasper.

Crystals are characterised by their shape, or rather structural design expressed in it. This is responsible for the optical and mechanical grain of the gem and will reveal itself even in a water-worn pebble that has lost its crystalline form. This grain must be ascertained before the cutting if the job is to be done satisfactorily.

In addition to what may be described as 'regular gemstones' certain minerals, not normally regarded as such, may occasionally achieve sufficient transparency and beauty of colour to be cut and polished. Cassiterite, scheelite, rutile, certain varieties of felspar and sphalerite (zinc blende) are in this category.

Most gemstones are of natural origin, but nowadays many gem minerals can be produced artificially. The crystallisation of diamond from the common forms of carbon requires great heat and pressure, and the technique of growing large crystals has not been successfully mastered yet. But small diamonds of gem quality, as well as the lower-grade industrial material are regularly manufactured. Large rubies, sapphires, emeralds and spinels, on the other hand, can be produced with relative ease; but, although such synthetic gems are often of the highest quality, their market value is low as compared even with inferior natural stones.

Synthetic gemstones include species of great beauty that do not appear to occur in nature at all, or, if so, remain undiscovered. Thus boron nitride (BN), or borazon, is a gem comparable to and harder than diamond; silicon carbide (Si_3C), familiar in the crude form of abrasive, is another similar gem, a shade softer than diamond, but exceeding it in fire; so too, are synthetic rutile and strontium titanate ($SrTiO_3$), which are comparatively soft.

A few materials regarded as gems are of organic origin, contemporary or fossil. Jet has already been mentioned, but amber, which is a fossil resin, is likewise of vegetable extraction; while pearl, coral and ivory (both of which may be fossil) are animal. Silicified or opalised wood and a few other fossils may also make attractive objects when cut and/or polished, and so properly belong in this company.

2

SOME IMPORTANT
PROPERTIES OF MINERALS

HARDNESS, SCRATCH AND STREAK

HARDNESS HAS BEEN REPEATEDLY MENTIONED IN THE PRECEDING chapter as a qualification of a mineral aspiring to 'gemhood'. It is not to be confused with toughness, for very hard substances are often brittle and can be readily shattered by a smart blow or crushed by heavy pressure. Diamond may be the hardest mineral known in nature, but laying it on an anvil and hitting it with a hammer will reduce it to crumbs. Clearly this is not the way to test the hardness of a valuable gem!

Hardness is one of the identification marks of a mineral species, although it may vary within narrow limits depending on minor fluctuations in chemical composition and some other factors. In some crystals it may further vary according to direction. Thus kyanite is also known as disthene, which is the Greek for 'two-strength', because its hardness on Mohs' scale is seven crosswise but only five lengthwise.

Just as an unknown length is measured by comparing it to a known length, say an inch, a centimetre or a light-year, so is hardness described in terms of other hardnesses. But the relationship is somewhat different, for hardness is not an additive property: we cannot add two equal hardnesses to each other to get a double hardness in the same way as we add miles or inches. To make a measurement of hardness comparable to that of length, it must be expressed in terms of an additive property; for instance, in terms of the pressure needed to produce an inelastic deformation in a 'spherical segment' of the tested mineral. Technical scales of hardness based on such methods do exist. The necessary tests, however, are difficult to apply in practice, and the rather crude old system devised by the German mineralogist Friedrich Mohs (1773–1839) continues to hold the field.

This method is based on a scratching sequence and the *mineralogical scratch* is produced by drawing a sharp point of one mineral over a clean, sound surface of another with a minimum of pressure. The harder mineral will leave a scratch on the softer one, but the softer will only mark it with its streak, which is a trail of its crushed substance. A scratch will continue to show after the scratched surface has been wiped clean, a streak will not. It is possible to obtain a kind of scratch with a somewhat softer material on a harder one if sufficient pressure is applied to crush it, but this is on par with smashing a diamond on an anvil.

For the sake of comparison, Mohs has arranged ten minerals in the order of increasing hardness, so that any mineral in his scale will be scratched by any of those that follow and will itself scratch all that precede it; and thus we have:

	Grade
Talc (or soapstone)	1
Gypsum (or rock salt)	2
Calcite	3
Fluorspar (fluorite)	4
Apatite	5
Orthoclase felspar	6
Quartz	7
Topaz (or spinel)	8
Corundum	9
Diamond	10

As already mentioned, borazon (crystalline boron nitride, BN) is harder than diamond, but so far has never been found in natural state. The main objection to Mohs' scale, however, is that the hardness differences between its successive steps are very uneven when measured by scientific methods. Thus diamond is some 140 times harder than corundum, while the gap between felspar and quartz corresponds to a ratio of barely 25:30. To deal with this, it is often necessary to interpolate further minerals between the markers of the scale and assign to them fractional hardness: for instance, sphene is $5\frac{1}{2}$; chalcedony, olivine and epidote $6\frac{1}{2}$; tourmaline $7\frac{1}{4}$; andalusite $7\frac{1}{2}$; beryl $7\frac{3}{4}$; and chrysoberyl $8\frac{1}{2}$. The synthetic materials, silicon carbide and boron carbide, important as abrasives in lapidary work but also known in the guise of gems, fall between corundum and diamond. Boron nitride powders are not commercially available at the time of writing (1972), but would no doubt make superlative abrasives.

Mohs hardnesses of some common objects are: fingernail, about 2; copper coin, 3; window glass, 5; penknife, between $5\frac{1}{2}$ and 6; and steel file, $6\frac{3}{4}$.

Where hardnesses are repeatedly tested it may be useful to make a set of hardness pencils. A hardness pencil is basically a holder mounting a pointed piece of appropriate mineral at the end—just like a pencil. It is economical to make it two-sided. The hardness grade should be marked on the holder, which may be of any suitable material to hand: wood, metal tubing or plastic, eg old ballpoint-pen holders with the ends cut off. The mineral bit can be secured to the holder with a plastic adhesive, Plastic Padding, or with dopping wax (see p 86), etc, and sharpened upon a lap or sanding wheel as and when necessary.

The streak, which may be described as the shadow of the scratch, is another useful aid to identifying minerals. Most crystals yield white powder when crushed, and so their streak is white, regardless of their colour. But the streak of fluorite is colourless, and many massive minerals have distinctive streaks, often quite different from their overall colour. Thus haematite is iron-grey when undecayed, but its streak is cherry-red; pyrite resembles gold and has been nicknamed 'Fool's Gold', but its streak is greenish-black, whereas that of real gold is golden. A plate of hard ceramic may be used as a 'streak-plate', or else a piece of fine carborundum paper will serve as it will take any mineral short of diamond and boron carbide.

SPECIFIC GRAVITY

Specific gravity, or density, may be defined as the weight of a body of any given substance divided into the weight of the same volume of water; or, since one cubic centimetre of water at 4°C weighs one gramme, as the weight of one cubic centimetre of this substance expressed in grammes. The specific gravity of water is one.

This property is *specific,* and so characteristic of a species of substance, such as a mineral, thus offering a clue to its identity. Like hardness, density may fluctuate somewhat in the same mineral species with the permissible variation in its chemical composition and degree of compactness, which depends on its origin. It will be understood that any cavities in the solid body of the specimen must not be included in the count.

The way of determining the specific gravity of a mineral is implicit in the definition of this concept: its weight must be compared to the weight of the same volume of water. For this purpose the specimen is first weighed in air and then suspended from the scale (which may have to be raised for this purpose) and immersed in water. As Archimedes has discovered, a body immersed in water is the lighter by the weight of the water it displaces, and so, if fully immersed, by the weight of the equal volume of water. If we call the weight-in-air A, that when fully immersed in water B, then the weight of the equal volume of water will be $C = A - B$, and so the density

$$D = \frac{A}{C} = \frac{A}{A-B}.$$

To take an example, we may weigh a specimen in air and find that it weighs 3·50oz ($A = 3·50$). If we then find that its weight when fully immersed in water is 2·18oz ($B = 2·18$), the calculation will show that the density D is approximately 2·65, and the material is most probably pure quartz.

A steelyard may be used instead of a scale balance. In a steelyard a weight to be measured is hung at a fixed point on the one side of the pivot about which the yard balances and is balanced by a single known weight sliding along the other side of the yard. Equilibrium is restored and the yard lies horizontal when the moments of the two weights become equal. The moment of a force—in this case a weight—is equal to its size times the distance of its point of application (to the beam) from the pivotal point. The sliding weight being known and the arm of the unknown weight fixed, the latter can be determined by moving the former to and fro along an appropriately calibrated scale.

In our second definition specific gravity, or SG for short, is expressed in grammes. It is, therefore, convenient to have the sliding weight similarly expressed. One gramme (g) is too small and unhandy a quantity, but 1og is eminently suitable. If now the sliding weight balances an identical weight at the weighing point when at a distance D from the origin of the scale, this distance will correspond to 1og. If an unknown weight is balanced at ½D it will be 5g, if at 2D it will be 20g, and so on. Otherwise the procedure is the same as before: we weigh the specimen in air and in water, and SG $= \dfrac{A}{A-B}$.

Since, however, the weights are given in grammes, the volume of the specimen is numerically equal to A−B.

In a *Walker's steelyard* (Fig 1), which is useful for dealing with larger

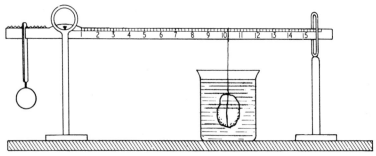

FIG 1 Walker's steelyard

specimens, the arrangement is reversed: the known weight is fixed in position and the specimen is moved along the scale. Suppose the reading of the scale is a for the specimen in air and b in water. These readings are inversely proportional to the corresponding weights, and we have:

$$SG = \frac{\frac{1}{a}}{\frac{1}{a}-\frac{1}{b}} = \frac{b}{b-a}.$$

It will be seen that the fixed weight does not appear in the formula at all, so that it can be varied to suit the specimen, nor need it be known.

A steelyard can be easily improvised with any suitable metal bar, eg a ruler, which is already graduated. It will need a hole to receive a pivot, say, a short length of stout wire or steel knitting needle, and a support for the pivot.

A quicker, if somewhat messy, way of finding the SG of a stone is by means of heavy liquids or a diffusion column. It is of more interest to a jeweller than to a lapidary, but is summarised below for the sake of completeness.

The heavy liquids commonly employed for this purpose are: Bromoform with SG 2·9 at room temperature; Methylene iodide with SG 3·33; and Clerici solution, which is a concentrated solution in water of thallium formate and thallium malonate, having an SG of up to 4·2. The latter is a colourless liquid, very expensive and poisonous. It can be diluted to any desired consistency. The other two liquids are non-poisonous and miscible with benzene or alcohol for dilution, but have to be kept in the dark, as they become strongly coloured if exposed to light for long.

The essence of the technique lies in that if the SG of a stone is less than that of the liquid the stone will float on the surface with partial immersion; if the two are equal the stone will be freely suspended at any level within the liquid; and, finally, if the stone is denser than the liquid it will sink to the bottom. The practice is to prepare solutions of different densities, corresponding to those of marker minerals and leave small pieces or crystals of the latter in free suspension in the beakers (or jars).

Thus a solution may be made to match the density of quartz, 2·65, and marked with a quartz crystal; another with the SG 3·06 of green tourmaline. The Clerici solution can be diluted to the density 4·00 of synthetic corundum or to the 3·52 of diamond.

A diffusion column is obtained by pouring some of a heavy liquid, such as the Clerici solution, into a tall beaker and filling up the rest of it with a lighter miscible liquid, such as water, very gently so as not to disturb the heavy liquid and to prevent mechanical mixing. The heavier liquid will gradually diffuse upwards into the lighter one above, yielding a column of graded density, from that of the pure heavy liquid at the bottom to that of the pure light liquid at the top. The density of the column can be graduated by letting small chips or crystals sink into it. Each of them will come to rest at the level corresponding to its SG, and will, moreover, keep this level as the density of the column alters owing to continued diffusion. Since, however, this is a very slow process, such a graduation will endure for many days and even weeks.

Given below is a table of the most important gemstones, arranged in the order of decreasing SG:

Mineral	SG	Mineral	SG
Cassiterite	7·0–6·8	Spodumene	3·20–3·15
Strontium Titanate	5·13	Andalusite	3·18–3·12
Zircon	4·7–3·94	Fluorspar	3·18–3·02
Almandine Garnet	4·3–3·9	Tourmaline	3·15–3·00
Rutile	4·26–4·18	Nephrite	3·0–2·9
Spessartine Garnet	4·20–4·12	Lapis Lazuli	2·9–2·7
Corundum	4·01–3·99	Turquoise	2·8–2·6
Demantoid Garnet	3·86–3·81	Beryl	2·80–2·68
Pyrope Garnet	3·8–3·7	Labradorite	2·70–2·66
Chrysoberyl	3·74–3·64	Sunstone	2·67–2·65
Kyanite	3·68–3·60	Quartz	2·65
Spinel	3·65–3·58	Cordierite	2·65–2·58

Topaz	3·56–3·50	Chalcedony	2·63–2·58
Sphene	3·53–3·45	Moonstone	2·57–2·56
Diamond	3·53–3·51	Orthoclase	2·57–2·55
Epidote	3·50–3·35	Amazonite	2·57–2·55
Olivine	3·46–3·35	Opal	2·2–1·9
Idocrase	3·4–3·3	Meerschaum	2·0–1·0
Jadeite	3·4–3·3	Jet	1·35–1·30
Diopside	3·31–3·27	Amber	1·1–1·05
Apatite	3·22–3·17		

CRYSTAL FAMILIES

Crystalline minerals assume a great variety of shapes. For example, calcite displays about 300 crystal forms, but they are all based on the same hexagonal design, rooted in its molecular structure. All crystals can be arranged in six systems, or families: cubic or isometric; tetragonal; hexagonal; orthorhombic; monoclinic; and triclinic.

The crystal systems are defined in terms of structural or crystallographic axes. These are not the same as geometrical axes of symmetry, although a plane passing through a crystallographic axis will divide a well-formed crystal into halves that can be brought into coincidence by rotation. A crystal, however, may have other axes of geometrical symmetry which are not its crystallographic axes, eg a cubic crystal may have as many as thirteen geometrical axes of symmetry, but only three of these are crystallographic. Moreover, a geometrical axis has no dimensions: it is only a direction. But a crystallographic axis is measured from intercept to intercept, ie between its points of intersection with two opposite faces of the crystal. Thus it has a definite length, and the ratios of the lengths of the axes are fixed for every type of crystal of a given mineral. For a full explanation the reader must be referred to textbooks of mineralogy.

Even then the crystal shapes illustrated in such works are ideals that are seldom realised in practice. Real crystals become jumbled, smaller ones sprout on the sides of large ones, and they may run out of material, etc. As a result considerable experience may be

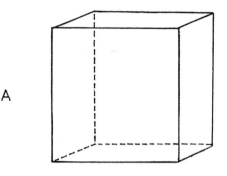

A

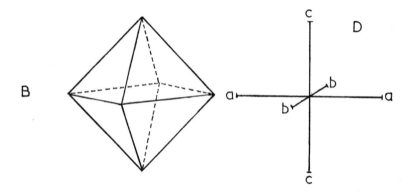

B

D

C

C

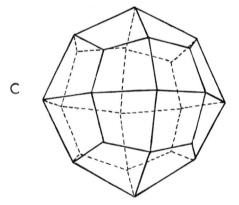

FIG 2 Cubic system: A = cube; B = octahedron; C = trapezo-
hedron (Leucite); D = crystallographic axes, aa = bb = cc,
all angles 90°

needed to recognise them for what they are. One way of acquiring such experience is by studying mineralogical collections in museums. But even experienced mineralogists make mistakes, and this is where other tests of identity such as hardness, streak, SG, fracture, cleavage, lustre, colour, etc, are useful.

The cubic system (Fig 2), is the most readily identifiable in natural specimens, for there are three crystallographic axes of equal length, at right angles to each other. They are pictured as lines joining the centres of the opposite sides of a cube, which is the simplest embodiment of this arrangement. But it can be developed into a tetrahedron, an octahedron, which still have three equal, mutually perpendicular axes, and various more complicated geometrical solids whose number of faces is some multiple of four. Moreover, the edges may be bevelled or depressed, the points cut off by small facets; the crystals may have pyramidal projections or depressions on the main faces, or just bulge out, as is often the case in diamond, which belongs to this family. All cubic crystals, however, may be described as symmetrical beads. The beads are isometric (the alternative name of the system), or of equal measure, because the distance between any pair of diametrically opposite apices (points) is always the same, so that the whole can be inscribed in a sphere.

This is a very numerous family, and contains, apart from diamond, all garnets, spinel, fluorite, native gold, silver and copper, as well as iron pyrite, galena and some other metal sulphides.

The tetragonal system (Fig 3) is as though the cubic elongated one way. One axis is longer than the other two, so that the crystal yields a square in cross section and in its simplest form a rectangle in long section; in other words it would be a square column. Such simplicity, however, is very rare, for most crystals in this family are prisms with pyramidal or like endings to the long axis, and may or may not have a square girdle, as well as various secondary facets and 'embellishments'. We must forget all this and mind the axes.

The family includes zircon, rutile, scheelite, cassiterite, chalcopyrite, etc.

The hexagonal system (Fig 4) is like the tetragonal, only the cross

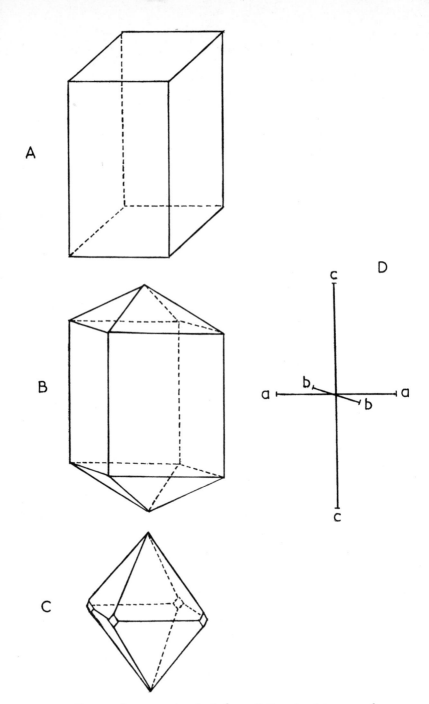

FIG 3 Tetragonal system: A = basic form; B, C = developments of the basic form; D = crystallographic axes, $aa = bb \neq cc$, all angles 90°

Page 23 Corundum has a wide range of colourings, as shown here. The red variety is the ruby, stones of any other colour are referred to as 'sapphire'. Both belong to the hexagonal system, but crystals of ruby tend to be tabular, those of sapphire columnar or spindle-shaped

Page 24 Zircon too occurs in a wide range of colours. It crystallises in the tetragonal system as exemplified here, and may be cut in brilliant or in step

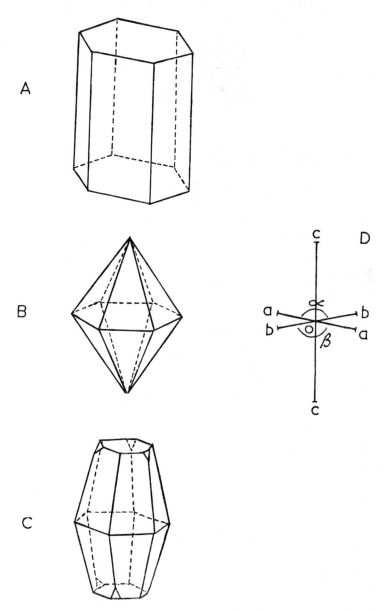

FIG 4 Hexagonal system: A = basic form (beryl); B = bipyramid
(quartz); C = 'barrel' (sapphire); D = crystallographic axes,
$aa = bb \neq cc$, $\measuredangle\ aOc = \measuredangle\ bOc = 90°$, $\alpha = \beta = 120°$

section is six-sided (the number of side faces may be doubled or effectively halved, eg in tourmaline). Thus we have one long axis and three (usually) short ones at right angles to it and intersecting successively at 120°. In its simplest form the crystal is a regular hexagonal column with flat endings, a shape that is not infrequent in beryl and nepheline. As a rule, however, the prism terminates in a pyramid at least at one end, or else the slanting terminal faces meet in a kind of 'roof'. The bottom edges of the terminal pyramid may be straight, ie at right angles to the long axis, or inclined. Sometimes there is no column, and the terminal pyramids meet each other. Minor faces may develop on the corners and/or along the edges. But the angles between the adjacent faces and that between the main terminal faces and the long axis are fixed in every mineral species.

Quartz, corundum, tourmaline, calcite and quite a few other minerals crystallise in this system.

The orthorhombic family (Fig 5) is an uneven variant of the tetragonal. All angles are still 90°, but the three axes are unequal in length, defining in the simplest case a brick-like solid. Once more such tabular crystals are comparatively rare; they occur, for instance, in prehnite. Natrolite is another fairly simple 'crystalliser' and often forms rectangular columns with pyramidal endings. In most cases, though, there are additional faces on the sides, so that the total number of vertical faces is some multiple of four (usually eight in topaz). The rule about angles mentioned in connection with the hexagonal system is universal and continues to apply. Crystals may be joined together, or twinned, in foursomes, yielding a cross, eg in staurolite.

In addition to those mentioned, olivine, hemimorphite and barytes are among the members of this family.

The monoclinic system (Fig 6) has the long axis sloping (angle $\neq$ 90°) to the plane of the two other unequal axes, which are still mutually perpendicular. The principle is clearly illustrated in the simple crystals of kunzite, a pink variety of spodumene, which are like an oblique brick, leaning one way. There are the usual complications. Orthoclase felspar, augite and hornblende are monoclinic.

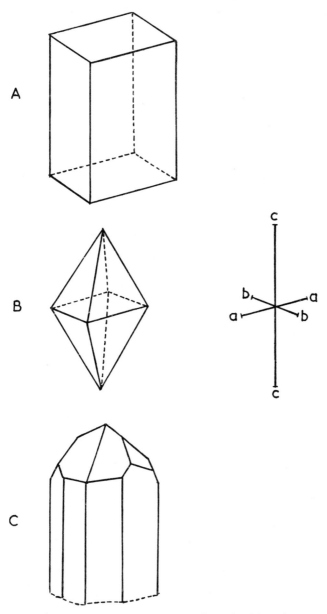

FIG 5 Orthorhombic system: A = basic form (andalusite); B = bipyramid (dyscrasite); C = complex prism (topaz); D = crystallographic axes, $aa \neq bb \neq cc$, all angles 90°

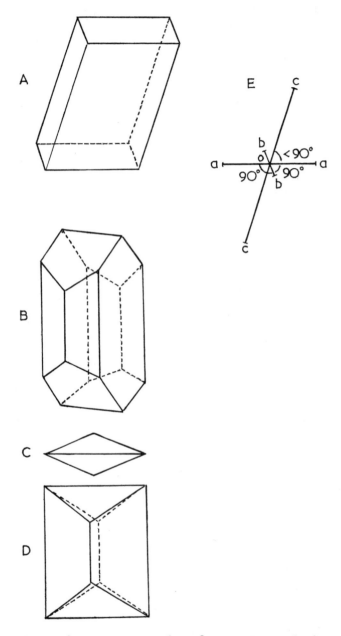

FIG 6 Monoclinic system: A = basic form; B, C, D = developments of the basic form; B = orthoclase (sanidine); C = sphene edge on; D = sphene from above; E = crystallographic axes, $aa \neq bb \neq cc$, $\measuredangle\, aOb = \measuredangle\, bOa = \measuredangle\, cOb = 90°$, $\measuredangle\, cOa \neq 90°$

The triclinic system (Fig 7), which includes the plagioclase felspar, has unequal axes which intersect at angles other than 90°. In the simplest embodiment, such as may be found in kyanite, the crystal is a kind of brick that will be leaning sideways, regardless of how it is stood up—a geometrical solid bounded by six parallelograms and glorying in the name of parallelepipedon. Axinite and rhodonite also belong to this system.

Crystals may have other distinctive structural features, useful for identification, as well as important in handling. Many crystals are lined, or striated, in a characteristic way. Quartz prisms are often lined across, while the somewhat similar hexagonal prisms of beryl have lengthwise striations. The latter is also a distinguishing mark of topaz. Axinite is strongly grooved, like corrugated cardboard. The faces of some other crystals display typical 'etchings'.

Minerals (whether crystalline or not) also differ in surface lustre. This may be metallic (like polished metal) in some opaque crystals; adamantine, as in diamond; vitreous, or glassy, which corresponds to reduced brilliance. Garnets have a resinous look. Some felspars are silky. Turquoise, chalcedony and jasper have a waxy appearance. The 'soapiness' of calcite to the touch is a related property.

Cleavage is a very important crystalline attribute. Some crystals can be readily split along certain planes parallel to their faces or axes. This property is particularly noticeable in mica and molybdenite, which form 'books' dividing into 'leaves' as though pages. But topaz, too, splits easily at right angles to the long axis of the prism, which may help to eliminate the unwanted parts of a crystal in the cutting, but must otherwise be guarded against. Diamond has well-developed cleavage along its main faces, which is again made use of in 'bruting', or rough-shaping the stone for cutting. When a stone is being facetted, however, the facets must be cut at an acute angle to the cleavage planes, as otherwise it will tend to peel off in layers.

Where cleavage is present the crystal will break 'clean' along its planes, though not across them. But even in the absence of cleavage minerals break with a characteristic fracture, which gives an additional

29

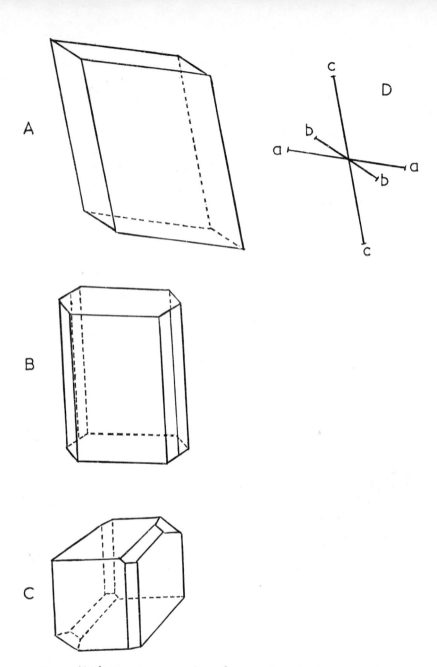

FIG 7 Triclinic system: A = basic form; B, C = developments; A = kyanite, C = axinite; D = crystallographic axes, $aa \neq bb \neq cc$, no angle = 90°

clue to their identity, although it would, of course, be wasteful to break a crystal of a valuable gemstone simply to examine the fracture. One of the commonest types of fracture is conchoidal, yielding a concentrically tiered surface as on a sea-shell (conch). Common glass, quartz and beryl fracture in this way. Amethyst, however, although a variety of quartz, has a related but distinctive rippled fracture. In topaz the fracture has a pearly lustre. Such terms as hackly (jagged) and splintery are self-descriptive. Breaks of this kind (agate, chalcedony) are obviously unfavourable to lapidary work.

3

THE OPTICS OF GEMS

THE INGREDIENTS OF FIRE

THE APPEAL OF A CUT GEM IS TO THE EYE, AND SO, SHAPE AND POLISH apart, must rely on the optical properties of the material, such as transparency, fire and colour. Gemstones may be opaque or translucent, but the most highly prized of them are transparent. We speak of a 'gem of purest water'. A diamond shines and sparkles with rainbow beams: this is fire, which together with relative rarity, a high price and the durability arising from great hardness, makes it a gem of gems. The synthetic upstarts: borazon, strontium titanate and colourless rutile owe their beauty to superior fire; and among the natural species cassiterite, also known as 'diamond tin', sphene and zircon come close to diamond in this property. The emerald's distinction, however, lies chiefly in its superb colouring, as it is not remarkable for its fire.

The main ingredients of fire are *refraction* and *dispersion* which is differential refraction according to colour, with a further contribution from double refraction, or *birefringence*, often associated with shifting colour, or *pleochroism*, which may be Englished as 'more-colouredness' and stems from the polarization of light.

Light moves at different speeds in different optical media (the textbook velocity of light refers to perfect vacuum), as a result of which a ray of light obliquely entering one medium from another is bent, or refracted. A straight stick partly immersed in water appears broken at the point where it crosses the surface of water. In our case the media are air and gemstone.

Consider a face of a crystal or of a cut gem struck by a thin ray, or pencil, of light.

Let us draw a line perpendicular, or normal, to the face at the point marked by the pencil, or the point of incidence. The angle between the ray and the normal is the angle of incidence, and the angle between the refracted (bent) ray in the stone and the extension of the normal into the stone is the angle of refraction. If the ray is incident upon the face at right angles (angle of incidence $= 0°$) there will be no refraction: it will pass on in a straight line. But if the incidence is other than vertical the light will be refracted in such a way that the ratio of the sines of the two angles, which corresponds to the ratio of the velocities of light in the two media, stays constant. This constant ratio is the refractive index, or RI for short, of the mineral in question.

We may call the angle of incidence a and that of refraction β. Then $RI = \dfrac{\sin a,}{\sin \beta}$ or $\dfrac{a'a''}{b'b''}$ (Fig 8). Light moves faster in the air than in the stone, so that the pencil of light is bent towards the normal, ie β is less than a, and RI is more than 1. But the situation is reversed when light passes from the stone into the air; it is as if the same diagram were viewed upside down. This must be so, since the ratio of velocities is inverted, and so, too, will be the index of refraction, becoming $\dfrac{1}{RI}$. β and a have changed their roles.

Clearly as β increases it must reach a value at which $a = 90°$ and the refracted ray glides along the inner face of the stone as shown by A'' (Fig 9). When this limiting value is exceeded the light will be bent back into the stone. This is called total internal reflection, and the angle at which it occurs is the *critical angle*.

It is this critical angle that is measured by the optical instrument called a refractometer, to obtain the RI. There is a further complication that an oil of a high RI is interposed between the gem and the glass hemisphere on which it is laid, so that the reflection takes place at the boundary between the stone and the oil. But a lapidary will not be generally required to determine the refractive indices of minerals, and should he decide to do so and purchase a refractometer he will find the necessary instructions in the manufacturer's leaflet.

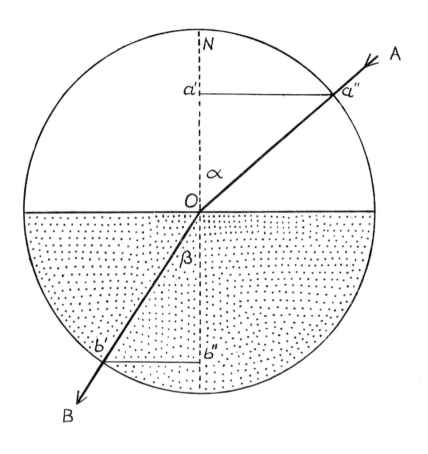

FIG 8 Refraction of light at air-stone interface (stone is stippled):
AO = incident ray; OB = refracted ray; α = angle of incidence; β = angle of refraction; NO = normal to interface at
$$\text{point of incidence; RI} = \frac{\sin \alpha}{\sin \beta} = \frac{a'a''}{b'b''}$$

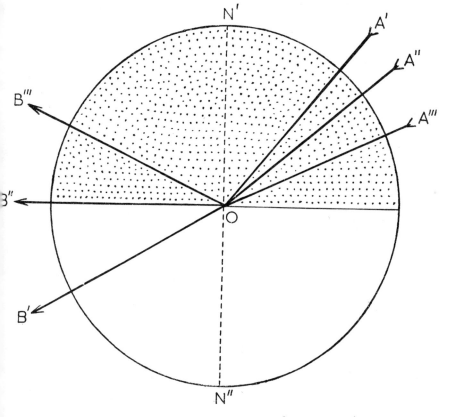

FIG 9 Total internal reflection at stone-air interface (stone is stippled): N'ON'' = normal at point of incidence O; A' refracted as B'; A'' at critical angle of incidence refracted as B''; A''' totally reflected as B'''

On the other hand, total internal reflection is of the greatest importance in facetting transparent gems. The critical angle can be obtained from the RI by simple mathematics, which will be found on p 191. The critical angles of the most important gemstones are listed in the table at the end of this chapter.

The principal types of cut and the techniques of facetting are considered in detail further on in the book, but basically in most types of cut we have a top part, called the crown, with a large horizontal facet known as the table, and a variously facetted lower part called the pavillion.

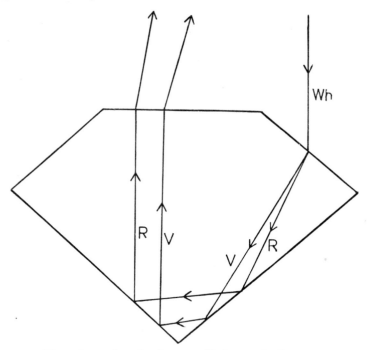

FIG 10 Dispersion and total reflection of light in a brilliant: Wh = white light; R = red; V = violet

To show the natural fire of a stone to the best advantage, the light entering the stone from above should be trapped in it and reflected back into the viewing eye. For this purpose the side facets of the pavillion must exceed the critical angle for the light coming down vertically through the table. There is always some reflection, but if the angles of the facets fall below the critical angle most of the light will pass through the stone, while the light coming in from below will be refracted towards the normal and pass out through the top of the gem, so that it can be seen through, like a kind of distorting lens. This is known as a 'fish-eye'.

It will be appreciated that the higher the RI, the more readily internal reflection will occur, thus enhancing the fire, with the practical consequence that the pavillion facets can be less steep and the stone need not be cut so deep.

But there is more to the fire than that. White light is a mixture of light of all (or some) colours, as demonstrated by Newton's glass prism (of triangular cross section) which split the light of the sun into a rainbow band (or spectrum)—and indeed by the rainbow itself. This is due to differential refraction, the violet light being refracted the most strongly and the red light—the least, the other colours being betwixt and between according to the rainbow sequence. Thus no precise value can be assigned to the refractive index unless the colour (or wavelength) of light be specified. This is conventionally taken as the yellow light of glowing sodium vapour, as in the sodium street lamps, approximately at the centre of the solar spectrum, which also corresponds to its maximum energy and the greatest colour sensitivity of the human eye.

The degree to which white light is split into its component colours varies from gemstone to gemstone, and not necessarily concurrently with the refractive index. This dispersive power, or dispersion, is measured by the difference between the RIs for the violet and red light respectively. The two indices for diamond are 2·451 and 2·407, so that it has a dispersion of 0·044; but it is 0·057 in demantoid garnet and 0·051 in sphene. The dispersion of synthetic rutile exceeds that of diamond several times and accounts for its extraordinary fire. Strontium titanate is likewise superior to diamond in this respect.

Birefringence, or double refraction, is another effect contributing to fire.

BIREFRINGENCE AND PLEOCHROISM

Light consists in electro-magnetic oscillations at right angles to the direction of propagation (beam of light). In ordinary unpolarised light these oscillations take place at all sorts of angles, and may be compared to bristles in a chimney-sweep's brush. In many crystals, however, the speed at which light travels depends not only on its colour (wavelength), but also on the direction of its oscillation, being different for oscillations along the intersecting axes of symmetry.

When light enters such a crystal it is polarised. Every oscillation is split into two component movements along the axes, so that a ray of light is doubled. Each of the two rays travels at a different speed, which will correspond to a different RI. The rays will be unequally deflected and separate, yielding a double image. Just as the dispersion of a gem is measured by the difference between its RIs for violet and red, so is birefringence a difference of the maximum and minimum refractive index (and so the maximum and minimum separation of the two rays) due to polarisation.

Calcite has a birefringence of 0·172, which is above that of most minerals, though in synthetic rutile it reaches the figure of 0·280. Sphene with 0·134 is also high on the list. In other gemstones the birefringence is much lower, and may not be readily detectable without a polarimeter, which is what the instrument used to measure polarisation is called. This most commonly consists of two rotatably mounted calcite prisms, known as Nicol prisms, or simply Nicols. If light passing through a singly refracting stone is viewed through crossed Nicols it will be stopped, however the stone is turned; with a birefringent stone there will be four positions of light and darkness. Anyway if we lay a suitably cut plate of calcite (Iceland spar) on a printed page the text will be doubled.

It will be readily seen that birefringence will tend to multiply internal reflections and so add to the fire. It may also be utilised in the cutting for special effects. On the other hand, weak birefringence yields fuzzy images, and so should be suppressed if possible. Some crystals contain needle-like inclusions, whose image can be multiplied by internal reflection, to form a kaleidoscopic pattern. Quartz is often pierced by needles of tourmaline and thin hairs of rutile, known as *flèches d'amour* (arrows of love), which may lend themselves to this treatment, but the birefringence of quartz is low—barely 0·009, and, therefore, unfavourable.

The same method is also employed to redeem unevenly coloured crystals, which applies more particularly to amethyst and kyanite. Not infrequently a good, clear crystal of amethyst is nearly colourless with an intense blob of burning violet at the turbid base. If this blob is suitably placed in the cut gem the colour can be spread all over it.

Birefringence may be associated with pleochroism (p 32), which most commonly reduces itself to dichroism, or 'two-colouredness', the two polarised rays differing not only in refractive index, but also in colour. Once more dichroism is not simply proportional to birefringence. For instance, cairngorm, or smoky quartz, while only weakly birefringent, is distinctly dichroic. On the other hand, zircon, with a birefringence of 0·059, is not noticeably dichroic.

Pleochroism is beautifully illustrated by cordierite. A crystal of an overall grey-blue colour appears a deep signal-blue when viewed along the prism of orthorhombic structure, but a pale yellow and nearly colourless across it and along the two minor axes. In tourmalines the colour does not change, but its intensity differs greatly with the angle of viewing, being very strong parallel to the long axis and weak across it. This property, too, is utilised in cutting, pale stones being cut with the table across the prism, to enhance the colouring, and dark ones with the table along the main axis, to brighten them up. Intermediate inclinations will give intermediate effects.

In most cases, however, the dichroism is too weak to warrant such treatment, though it may serve as an aid to identification by means of an optical instrument called a *dichroscope*, where the stone can be examined under various angles. One of its main applications in jeweller's work is in distinguishing between cut specimens of true emerald and other green stones. This can be done much more simply with a Chelsea filter, which transmits only a yellow-green and a red part of the spectrum. When seen through such a filter, the emerald will look red, whereas other stones remain green. Synthetic blue spinel behaves similarly to emerald.

Dichroism is destroyed by heating, which provides a way of weeding out stones whose colour has been changed by heat treatment, as is done with citrines (obtained from brown or amethyst quartz) and topaz (which turns pink). Jeweller's glass, known as *paste*, or in better imitations as *strass*, is likewise devoid of dichroism, even when its fire has been enhanced by an admixture of lead or thallium. Gemstones are also better conductors of heat than glass and so feel colder to the touch.

Other amorphous materials behave similarly to glass in this respect, although a weak dichroism may be induced in them if they are subjected to stress. Minerals that crystallise in the cubic system are singly refracting and so non-dichroic as well. For this reason they are known as (optically) isotropic, ie the same in all directions. Yet even in other crystal families the two polarised rays coincide along an optic axis, which corresponds to vertical incidence on the polarising plane (p 38). In the tetragonal and hexagonal system there is only one such axis, and they are known as uni-axial. The remaining three systems (orthorhombic, monoclinic and triclinic) have two optic axes with three refractive indices and are called biaxial. The optic axes coincide with at least some of the structural (symmetry) axes of the crystal.

The tables give two values for the RI of birefringent minerals, corresponding to the two polarised rays. For instance, rutile is doubly refracting with indices 2·90 and 2·62, but diamond and strontium titanate are cubic and singly refracting with RIs 2·42 and 2·41 respectively. The refractive index may, like other properties, also vary within the same species owing to minor fluctuations in chemical composition and mode of origin, which are often associated with colour. This is particularly true of garnets and zircons, but morganite, which is a pink or lilac variety of beryl also has a somewhat higher RI of 1·59–1·58 than other beryls (emerald, heliodor, aquamarine), which are only up to 1·58–1·57.

Page 41 Topaz (left) and tour-maline (right). The crystals of topaz are orthorhombic and have a narrower range of colourings than corundum or zircon; the hexagonal prisms of tourmaline occur in a number of colours, sometimes present in one and the same crystal. Owing to an unequal development of side facets, the latter often approximate to a triangle in cross-section

Page 42 Lapis lazuli, scapolite and felspar. The oriental goblet is lapis lazuli, the green crystal and tear-drops are amazonite, the shimmering, carved, blue stone is labradorite. The step-cut yellow and pinkish stones on the left are scapolite, but the similar yellow stone on the right is a transparent variety of orthoclase felspar from Madagascar. The cabochon in the pin is sunstone, and the colourless brilliant above it is adularia. Moonstones are on the extreme right. Some of the cabochons display the property of chatoyancy or adularescence

COLOUR AND OTHER OPTICAL PROPERTIES

As previously indicated (p 10), the colouring of a stone is no sure guide to its mineralogical identity. In some species, such as the garnets, the colour is closely associated with the chemical composition, which in turn forms the basis of classification, therefore if we have a purplish-red garnet we can be sure that it is an almandine. Similarly a yellowish-green garnet is certainly a demantoid. Olivine, too, may be relied upon to be olive-green, but a rare red variety exists. In most cases, however, colour by itself may be highly misleading. For instance, quartz may be colourless (rock crystal), yellow (citrine), brown (cairngorm), smoky, black (morion), violet (amethyst), pink (rose quartz), flesh-pink to russet (ferruginous quartz), leek-green (prase), blue (sapphire quartz), or milky. Moreover, there is a Brazilian variety of amethyst that turns bright-green when heated and is then known as vermarine. Corundum, commonly known in the carmine-red guise of ruby and the blue of sapphire, also occurs in the colourless, green, yellow and violet form. Tourmaline may be of almost any colour, bar violet. Although diamond is typically colourless, it, too, may be blue, yellow or green depending on minor impurities. In fact, most gemstones are colourless when chemically pure.

It may happen that more than one colour is present in one and the same crystal. This effect is best known in tourmaline, where part-red, part-green and part-blue crystals are not uncommon, and other colour combinations are possible. Such crystals are often cut with the table along the prism, to show the different colours in a 'rainbow gem'; we will recall, however, (p 39) that some of the intensity of the colouring is lost in this arrangement. Beryl and topaz, too, are occasionally found in multicoloured crystals, those of beryl shading over from white at the base through yellow, green and blue into pink (morganite) at the tip. Some other minerals occasionally show similar colour variations, but it is more common for the colour to be graded from the base, where it is at its deepest, to the tip, where it is pale. This is particularly true of quartz.

Additional optical effects may be due to inclusions, internal fractures or structural peculiarities.

Aventurine felspar (sunstone) and aventurine quartz owe their sparkling, speckled appearance to the inclusions in the form of tiny plates of haematite and mica respectively. In rainbow quartz the light is split into rainbow colours on the reflecting surfaces formed by small internal fractures. Such stones are liable to break up into pieces if wrongly handled and should be carefully examined before cutting. The effect can be multiplied by internal reflection.

Some sapphires and rubies contain microscopic canals ranged along the minor axes of the hexagonal crystal, and, when cut *en cabochon* (a 'beetle' cut with a rounded top) with the greatest thickness of the gem in the long axis of the prism, display a six-rayed star of light. This effect is called *asterism*, and such gems are described as star-sapphires and star-rubies.

The *adularescence* of moonstone, a variety of potash felspar known as adularia, is a similar phenomenon due to reflection of light from tiny platy inclusions lying in the structural cleavage planes of the crystal (p 29). In a suitably oriented cabochon the cream-coloured translucent stone shows a moving area of bluish sheen. Fibrous inclusions are responsible for the *chatoyancy* (ie playfulness) in the form of a moving band of light in chrysoberyl and quartz 'cat's-eye', tiger-eye and other 'eyes', which are always cut as cabochon and never facetted.

In opaque stones colour is substantially a surface property, but even opaque stones are translucent in thin section, so that the difference between transparent, translucent and opaque material is one of degree only. Thus the beauty of an opaque stone may be more than skin-deep. *Schiller* (shimmer) of some felspars is a surface property, but in labradorite (a variety of plagioclase), it becomes iridescent owing to the interference of light reflected from structural planes exposed at an angle. Labradorite in the raw looks a dirty greenish-grey, and its play is revealed only by fracture or a suitably slanted cut facet. It is usually cut and mounted as a flat slab.

Opal is translucent and its play of colours is a similar effect, due to reflection from thin films within the stone. Such films may also develop in, or more frequently on, quartz crystals, and in the latter case would, of course, be destroyed by cutting.

Opal is usually cut *en cabochon* or flat, and not facetted, with the exception of fire opal, which may be sufficiently transparent for facetting.

Appended here is a table of optical properties of the more important gemstones. All properties vary within certain limits, sometimes broader, sometimes narrower, and to this extent excess of accuracy can be spurious. In most cases there are two figures giving the maximum and minimum values of the refractive index, which may be wholly or partly due to double refraction or to fluctuations in chemical composition, but the record can be set straight by taking birefringence into account. The maximum critical angle corresponds to the lowest value of RI, and so will ensure total internal reflection in every case. It is calculated with four-figure accuracy, but it must be appreciated that the smallest angle distinguishable to an unaided eye is about 2′, so that this accuracy is far in excess of practical requirements, and it is always better to err on the safe side by taking a larger angle. The arrangement is according to RI in decreasing order.

The RI of glass is comprised between 1·67 and 1·50, which corresponds to a maximum critical angle of 41° 47′. Being amorphous (toughened glass may be crystallised), glass is singly refracting. Opaque stones have been excluded from the list for obvious reasons.

A further property of some gemstones that may deserve mention in the present context is *fluorescence*, which consists in absorbing the invisible ultraviolet radiations and re-emitting their energy in the form of visible light, often of unearthly colours. This is a distinctive attribute of fluorspar, also known as fluor or fluorite, from which indeed the word fluorescence is derived. When illuminated with an ultraviolet lamp, fluorspar emits a deep 'velvet' violet glow, though some varieties fluoresce in other colours, or fail to fluoresce at all. In ordinary circumstances the effect is invisible, but sunlight does include an ultraviolet component, and it has been suggested that

45

Name	RI	Dispersion	Refraction	Birefringence
Synthetic Rutile	2·90–2·62	0·300	double	0·287
Diamond	2·42	0·044	single	nil
Strontium Titanate	2·41	0·175*	single	nil
Cassiterite	2·09–1·99	0·071	double	0·096
Sphene	2·06–1·91	0·051	double	0·150
Blue Zircon	1·97–1·92	0·038	double	0·070
Other Zircons	1·97–1·78	0·038	double	up to 0·059
Demantoid	1·90	0·057	single	nil
Almandine	1·81–1·75	0·024	single	nil
Spessartine	1·80		single	nil
Corundum	1·77–1·76	0·018	double	0·008
Epidote	1·77–1·73	0·028	double	0·035
Chrysoberyl	1·76–1·75	0·015	double	0·009
Pyrope	1·75–1·72	0·027	single	nil
Kyanite	1·73–1·72	0·011	double	0·016
Spinel	1·72	0·020	single	nil
Idocrase	1·72–1·71	v. low	double	0·004
Diopside	1·70–1·67	0·016	double	0·020–0·030
Olivine	1·69–1·65	0·020	double	0·038
Spodumene	1·68–1·66	0·017	double	0·015
Jadeite	1·67–1·65		double	0·013
Apatite	1·64–1·63	0·013	double	0·003
Andalusite	1·64–1·63	0·013	double	0·010
Tourmaline	1·64–1·62	0·017	double	0·018
Topaz	1·63–1·62	0·014	double	0·008
Nephrite (Jade)	1·63–1·61		double	0·025
Morganite	1·59–1·58	0·014	double	0·010
Beryl (Emerald etc)	1·58–1·57	0·014	double	0·005–0·009
Labradorite	1·57–1·56	0·012	double	
Quartz	1·55–1·54	0·013	double	0·009
Chalcedony	1·55–1·54		single	nil
Cordierite	1·55–1·54	0·014	double	0·008
Amber	1·54	v. low	single	nil
Orthoclase†	1·53–1·52	0·012	double	0·010
Opal	1·46–1·44		single	nil
Fluorspar	1·43	0·010	single	nil

* Approximately

† Including moonstone, adularia and sunstone

Critical Angle	Colour	Dichroism	(Hardness)
22° 33′	none	absent	$(6\frac{1}{2})$
24° 24′	variable	absent	(10)
24° 29′	none	absent	(6)
30° 2′	brown	distinct	$(6\frac{1}{2})$
31° 38′	brown, yellow, green	distinct	$(5\frac{1}{2})$
31° 23′	blue	strong	$(7\frac{1}{2})$
34° 13′	variable	unobservable	$(7\frac{1}{2}-6)$
31° 38′	green	absent	$(6\frac{1}{2})$
34° 45′	red to purple	absent	$(7\frac{1}{4})$
33° 39′	red	absent	$(7\frac{1}{4})$
34° 35′	variable	weak	(9)
35° 17′	yellow, brown, green	strong	$(6\frac{1}{2})$
34° 45′	yellow, green	weak	$(8\frac{1}{2})$
34° 55′	red	absent	$(7\frac{1}{4})$
35° 27′	mainly blue	distinct	$(7-5)$
35° 27′	red, orange, blue	absent	(8)
35° 48′	green	weak	$(6\frac{1}{2})$
36° 49′	green	very weak	$(6-5)$
37° 18′	olive, green, brown	weak	$(7-6\frac{1}{2})$
36° 58′	variable	weak	$(7-6\frac{1}{2})$
37° 18′	variable	weak	$(7-6\frac{1}{2})$
37° 45′	variable	distinct	(5)
37° 45′	yellow, brown	strong	$(7\frac{1}{2})$
38° 5′	variable	strong	$(7\frac{1}{2}-7)$
38° 5′	variable	distinct	(8)
38° 24′	white to green	weak	$(6\frac{1}{2}-5\frac{1}{2})$
39° 20′	pink to purple	weak	$(7\frac{3}{4})$
39° 26′	yellow, green, blue, colourless	weak	$(8-7\frac{1}{2})$
39° 55′	grey	absent	(6)
40° 30′	variable	distinct	(7)
40° 30′	variable	absent	$(6\frac{1}{2})$
40° 30′	blue	strong	$(7\frac{1}{2}-7)$
40° 30′	usually yellow, brown	absent	$(3-2\frac{1}{2})$
41° 4′	variable	absent	(6)
44° 1′	variable	absent	(6)
44° 14′	variable	absent	(4)

this may contribute to some special hues encountered in fluorspar. Scheelite fluoresces in lilac, and many other minerals exhibit this property to a less marked degree, which can be displayed to advantage in a special cabinet.

4

BEAUTY,
PLAIN AND FASHIONED

THE BEGINNINGS OF LAPIDARY ART

MINERALS AS FOUND IN NATURE ARE OFTEN VERY BEAUTIFUL. THERE IS an exquisite balance of form in a crystal, and even the departures from simple geometrical symmetry may add to its aesthetic appeal. People ignorant of crystallography often express surprise that so regular and attractive a structure could be the work of natural forces and not of a skilled lapidary. It seems a shame to interfere.

Indeed, it may sometimes be possible to mount a crystal in its natural state as a jewel, with just a little polishing work, to clean up its faces and bring out their lustre. This course was frequently followed in the historical past, before the art of cutting and facetting hard stones had been discovered and developed. Yet perfect crystals are comparatively rare; more often than not natural specimens are disfigured in some way or other, flawed, intergrown, partly transparent, or unevenly coloured, so that only a small fraction is suitable for jewellery.

In any case massive stones are formless in their natural state. Even the colour of opaque or translucent material does not show to advantage unless it is wet. It has to be cut and polished, to acquire tasteful shape and appear to be in a condition of permanent wetness. As we have already seen, such stones as labradorite have to be cut at an appropriate angle, to reveal their iridescent beauty. Yet a perfect transparent crystal, too, will gain by skilful facetting, which brings out its inherent fire, multiplies the internal reflections and/or enhances the colour.

49

Opaque and translucent stones whose appearance is determined mainly by their surface properties are usually cut into flat slabs or rounded surfaces, known under the French name of *cabochon*, although they may also be carved as *cameos* or *intaglios*—an ancient art that has lately gone out of fashion. Transparent material used to be given similar treatment in the past, and garnets are still occasionally cut *en cabochon*, being then known as 'carbuncles', which is a survival of the earlier practices.

The use of precious stones as personal ornaments in the form of cabochons or beads goes back to the first stirrings of civilisation. The early craftsmen generally preferred softer materials, such as jet or amber, but the ancient Egyptian lapidaries had mastered the technique of cutting, polishing and drilling into tubular beads such hard stones as agate; and Egyptian goldsmiths have left examples of tasteful jewellery, wrought of gold and precious stones, dating from 2000 BC onwards.

Engraved stones, to which alone the term *gem* properly applies, were known in Babylon and Niniveh and there are fine examples of this art from Greece from between 1000 and 700 BC. Theophrastus mentions engraved emeralds, although carving emeralds was deemed an offence.

In a *cameo*, for which onyx or sandonyx is used, figures or designs carved from a lighter layer stand out in low relief against a darker background, or the other way round, often with a very pleasing effect. In an intaglio, which is the Italian for 'cut-in', the design is a hollow carving in a flat face of a uniformly coloured stone.

In the Dark Ages of faith and fist that followed the collapse of the Western Roman Empire under the onslaught of barbarian hordes, all arts and crafts suffered an eclipse from which they were slow to emerge. Even so that darkness was not quite as thick and universal as is sometimes made out, and little lights continued to flicker here and there in the monastic cloisters. About the middle of the tenth century one Theophilus, tentatively identified as a Benedictine monk from Cologne, composed a Latin *Treatise on Divers Arts*, including the lapidary.

Some of his 'diverse' instructions are as bizarre as they are horrific. Thus 'if you want to carve a piece of rock crystal' you are enjoined to 'take a two- or three-year-old goat and bind its feet together and cut a hole between its breast and stomach, in the place where the heart is, and put the crystal in there, so that it lies in the blood until it is hot'. This was clearly a magical device, said briefly to soften the crystal and make carving easy. Since it could not conceivably have any such effect, the procedure had to be sustained, consuming an unspecified number of goats.

On the whole, however, Theophilus's teaching is sound. He recommends grinding the stone on hard sandstone, which comes close enough to the practices of Idar-Oberstein and to the modern sanding wheel, of which more in due course. The next stage was rubbing the stone against another of the same kind 'but finer and smoother'. 'Tile dust', moistened with saliva, on a lead plate and on an untanned goat skin were used for final polish. The stone was mounted on a 'long piece of wood' with chaser's pitch, which is the prototype of the dop. Sand lubricated with water was the natural abrasive used in Egypt and Babylonia; but Theophilus mentions emery, which is a form of corundum of grade nine on Mohs' scale and therefore adequate for anything short of diamond.

The art of stone engraving was revived in Western Europe, and Italy and France in particular, in the thirteenth century. After that the development was rapid. In England a famous school of gem engravers arose and flourished towards the end of the eighteenth century. It was attuned to the leisurely tempo of life in a pre-industrial aristocratic society. In an age of jet planes and space travel, general scramble for higher wages and profits, with tinned push-button pleasures, few can afford or are inclined to acquire the laborious skill of cutting cameos, and fewer still would be prepared to pay an adequate price for such objets d'art. However, automation marches on into a brave new world of greater leisure and broader culture. Hobbyism is increasing by leaps and bounds, and these trends may yet be reversed.

Be this as it may, the difficult art of carving and engraving gems

51

was mastered in remote antiquity, but the facetted stones with which we are familiar today are a comparatively recent historical arrival. The old Indian diamonds were mounted more or less as found, new polished facets being added to the natural crystal form only to remove blemishes. Otherwise cabochon was the rule.

The first crudely facetted stones appeared in Europe in the fourteenth century, but the modern epoch dawned in 1476, when Lodewyk van Berquem of Bruges, in Flanders, found that diamond could be cut and polished with diamond—an idea embryonically present in Theophilus's *Treatise*. This stimulated a rapid development in the art of facetting hard crystalline material, especially in the Low Countries, France and Germany, whence it was eventually brought to Britain by immigrants and refugees. All the conventional types of cut, still used today, had emerged before the close of the eighteenth century.

Nowadays we have synthetic gems and abrasives, machinery has been greatly improved and is driven by electric power instead of a treadle. Automation is increasingly employed in the cutting of cheaper semi-precious stones. But diamonds, emeralds and rubies are still left to the ancient skill or the lapidary's eye and hand, for which no satisfactory substitute has been found. Nor has there been any great change in the basic methods and products of this skill. This is not a matter of trade conservatism and mental inertia alone, for the traditional forms have a solid scientific basis in the properties of the minerals themselves. Still, many variations on the old themes are possible.

TRADITIONAL TYPES OF CUT

Historically the earliest, the simplest and the beginner's favourite pre-serve is the *simple cabochon*. It is a beetle type of cut, used for opaque or at most translucent stones, with a rounded top of varied curvature, high, low or medium. The flat base with which it is mounted in a ring or similar article is usually left unpolished. The edge of a cabochon may be chamfered, and there is nothing to prevent its

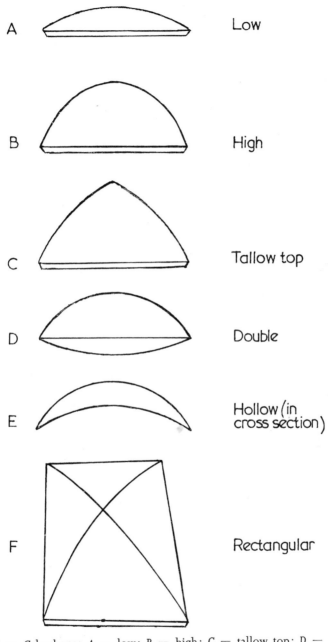

A   Low

B   High

C   Tallow top

D   Double

E   Hollow (in cross section)

F   Rectangular

FIG 11 Cabochons: A = low; B = high; C = tallow top; D = double; E = hollow; F = rectangular

being facetted. A flat slab, as in an engraved signet ring, may be regarded as a limiting case of the cabochon cut.

Sometimes the cabochon ends upwards in a blunt point or short ridge, known as *tallow-top*. It may also be cut square with diagonal ridges. Other similar developments are possible.

In a *double cabochon* both sides, top and bottom, are convex and polished. The underside is 'lower', or of smaller curvature, as a rule, but only a small step divides this type of cut from a round or ellipsoidal bead, which is indeed a development of the cabochon, except for being drilled for threading. The double cabochon cut is especially suitable for translucent stones.

In the *hollow cabochon* the bottom half is concave; it is like an inverted dish thickened in the middle. This form is used mainly with very dark, transparent or translucent stones, to admit more light. Normally, however, transparent stones are facetted. Star sapphires and rubies and chatoyant gems are the exception, and, as already mentioned, dark red garnets may be cut as carbuncle cabochons. Rock crystal makes attractive, sparkling balls.

On the other hand, metallic minerals, such as haematite and pyrite (marketed as marcasite), where the effect is due wholly to surface reflection, are usually facetted. Weakly translucent materials, eg chrysocolla and rhodonite, have also been facetted on occasion in recent years. This is largely a matter of taste and the particular effect, including the mounting, that is aimed at. A diamond cabochon, however, would be a solecism, even worse than a carved emerald.

The cut especially conceived to bring out the best in a diamond is the *standard brilliant*, first introduced by Petruzzi towards the end of the seventeenth century. As already adumbrated (p 36), in a brilliant we have two tapered parts, at the top and the bottom of the stone (as mounted), divided by the *girdle*, along which the stone is set. The top part is known as the *crown*, and the bottom one as the *pavillion* or *culasse*.

The conventional crown has thirty-three facets: the central large *table*, which is about half the diameter of the girdle, is octagonal, with *star facets* extending away from each side of the octagon. In the old-

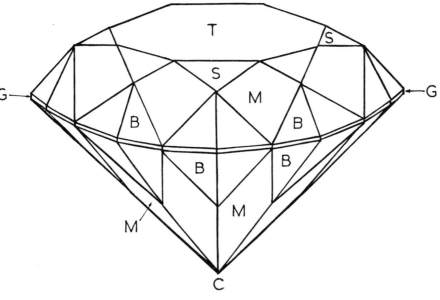

FIG 1 2 Standard brilliant cut (facet angles are those of a quartz gem) :
   T = table; S = star facet; B = break facet; M = main facet;
   C = culet

fashioned nomenclature there were templets or bezels, quoins or lozenges, skew and skill facets; nowadays, however, we need distinguish only the kite- (or deltoid-) shaped main facets, with the opposite points (apices) touching the table and the girdle respectively, and the break facets standing between these upon the girdle in pairs of right-angled triangles. Break facets are also known as girdle facets, which is somewhat misleading inasmuch as the girdle is itself facetted, to receive the crown and the pavillion break facets.

   In the pavillion below the girdle there are again sixteen break (cross) facets, which lead down to another eight main (pavillion) facets, composing the star pattern of the downward pyramid. It may, but need not, be cut short by the culet, which is a much diminished counterpart of the table, one-fifth of the girdle in diameter. This makes twenty-four or twenty-five facets altogether. If we bear in mind that every facet must be absolutely accurate in area and angles, and the arrangement may be easily spoiled by overcutting (ie cutting a facet for too long and so making it too large), we will see that cutting a brilliant is a highly skilled and difficult job.

The octagonal shape of the brilliant table derives from the cubic crystalline habit of diamond, but may not be equally suitable for other gems. The number of sides may be varied. Nor is there anything sacrosanct about the total number of facets. It is handier and more logical to have fewer of them in a small stone, and to increase their number in a large one.

Moreover, the shape just described is referred to as the round brilliant, meaning that the girdle and table are symmetrical and can be inscribed in a circle. But this shape may be variously deformed becoming elliptical instead of circular in outline, or even irregular for some special mounting design, or indeed to make the best possible use of the available clear material. An ellipse pointed at its two narrow ends yields a marquise, and if only one side is pointed we have a pendeloque, which, as the name suggests, is particularly suited to a pendant.

The distortions mentioned so far are horizontal only and do not otherwise affect the number and arrangement of facets, while the depth of the crown remains one half that of the pavillion. In a briolette, the gem is elongated vertically and may be said to consist of two pavillions: a low (shallow) one at the bottom and a high (deep) one at the top, usually without culets. A design of this kind is especially well adapted to earrings.

The brilliant cut and its derivatives have been devised to show up the fire in stones of high refractive index. When, however, the main attraction lies in the colour some form of step or trap cut is used. In this design we again have the crown and the pavillion, the table and the culet, but instead of being triangles, the break and main facets (if there is any point in distinguishing between them) are trapezia with long sides parallel to those of the table, the girdle and the culet,

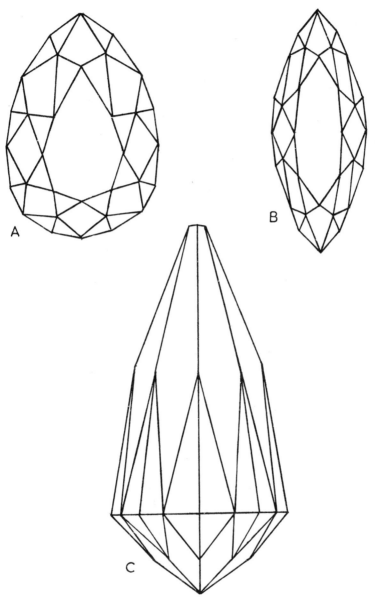

FIG 13 Developments of the brilliant: *A* = pendeloque;
  B = marquise; *C* = briolette

forming steps, which are widest at the girdle and decrease progressively up and down.

The *table cut* is the simplest embodiment of the idea with only one step between the girdle and table and culet respectively. More usually there are three steps in both the crown and the pavillion, the first crown step being very narrow. Most step-cut gems are square or rectangular, but in the *emerald cut*, which is especially deep to show

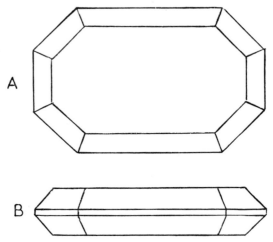

FIG 14 Table cut: A = crown or pavillion; B = side view

the colour, the shape is an elongated octagon. Any other polygon, an ellipse or a circle, will do as well, though what is normally known as the 'round step cut' has sixteen sides. In this case there is usually no culet and the pavillion is pointed.

A step cut is much easier than a brilliant, and there are various *mixed cuts*, embodying some features of both. In the simplest case we have the crown of a brilliant perched on a step pavillion, which allows us to combine the advantages of both types of treatment.

Another traditional form of cut is the *rose*. This may be described as a facetted single cabochon, inasmuch as the stone is flat at the bottom and convex upwards: it has no pavillion. The crown consists

Page 59 (above) Crystal-walled cavity or druse, about 3 × 10 ft. The crystals are calcite (dog-tooth spar), from Dulcote Quarry, Somerset, England; (below) massive and crystalline minerals: Cubical purple fluorite on calcite in the background, and a great mass of massive haematite (kidney ore) in the foreground from a display at the Carlisle Museum, Cumberland, England

Page 60 (*above*) Silicon-carbide grinding wheels of various sizes, 6in and 8in wide and $\frac{1}{4}-\frac{3}{4}$in and 1in thick; (*below*) laps made with various materials: tin, plastic, copper, plywood and gun metal

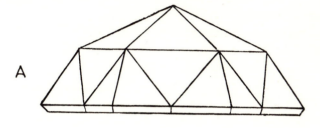

A

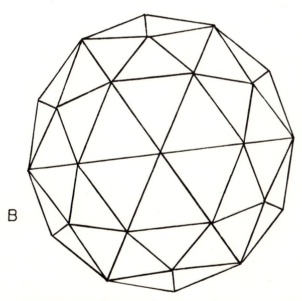

B

FIG 15 A = simple rose (side view, bevelled at base); B = double
    Dutch rose (from above)

of six low triangular facets, called *star facets*, composing a hexagon in plan view. From the sides of the hexagon six further triangular (main) facets extend down to the girdle (or base) of the stone. Between these lie twelve *cross* or *break facets*, the total of eighteen making up the so-called *dentelle*. The total number of facets is twenty-four, but there are many variants of this traditional design, including a *step rose*, having a small table and steps on its sides.

In a *double rose* there is a pavillion, which is likewise rose-cut. If the two roses are equally deep the result is a bead. I have a small cairngorm having the crown of a brilliant and a rose pavillion. Both the rose and the step can be developed into a briolette.

Rose cuts are used mainly for small stones. They have considerable brilliance, and the absence of a table may be utilised to conceal internal flaws. This cut is also well suited to minerals with a metallic lustre, but it does not wear well in a ring, especially with softer materials.

Briolettes may be transparent or opaque; they can be employed to advantage for displaying internal inclusions (eg *flèches d'amour* or tourmaline needles, see p 38); but their use is limited to gemstones of low refractive index.

SOME NEW WINE IN THE OLD BOTTLES

Ingenuity and creative imagination can be brought to bear on any traditional form, once the basic techniques have been mastered. There exists some prejudice against mixing cabochon and facetted cuts, possibly because in learning the art the progress is from cabochon to facet. Yet facets, either with sharp or rounded edges may at times be successfully introduced into a cabochon cut.

On the other hand, a large number of cuts have been evolved in modern times from Petruzzi's original brilliant, by both complicating and simplifying the arrangement of facets. There is the zircon cut with a double star in the pavillion, the double diamond where the main facets of the brilliant are horizontally or vertically split, and the enormously complex Portuguese and Scotch cuts. It may, however, be of greater interest to consider some simplified versions.

The *spinning wheel* cut has no table, no culet and no break facets. It thus represents a high degree of simplicity, although the number of facets is comparatively large; it is also very effective for low-refracting materials, such as quartz.

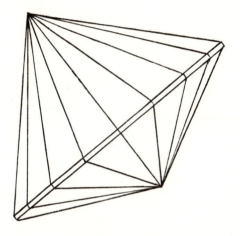

FIG 16 Spinning wheel cut of sixteenfold symmetry (side view)

For reasons that will become apparent later on, the pavillion is cut first and so we will begin at the bottom. We have here a number of isosceles triangles, arranged spokewise and suitably inclined to ensure internal reflection (an angle of $43°$ or so is recommended for quartz). There is a like number of girdle facets, interposed between the pavillion and the crown, which consists of an identical spoke pattern of isosceles triangles, cut at about $15°$ to the horizontal plane.

We find another simple and effective arrangement in the *commercial cut*, professionally used mainly for small stones. It has a table, but no culet and no star facets. Conventionally the symmetry is eightfold and the gem is 'round' (see p 56). Thus there are eight main facets and eight break facets in both the pavillion and the crown. The pavillion main facets are pencil-shaped, the point of the pencil

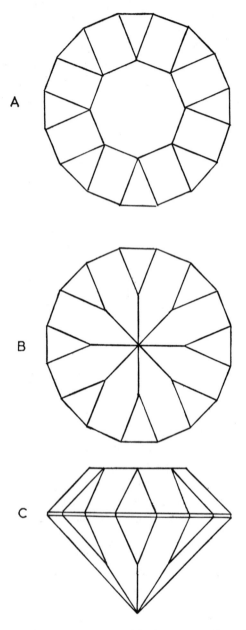

A

B

C

FIG 17 Commercial cut: A = crown (plan); B = pavillion (plan);
C = side view

being at the culet point, while the breaks are triangles, extending halfway and based on the girdle, over which they are adjacent to the identical facets in the crown. In the crown, however, the apex of the break touches the table, the mains on the two sides being rectangular. The inclination of the mains is the same in both halves of the gem, and the breaks are some 2° steeper.

The *petal cut* is a similar attractive scheme. Here, however, the pavillion mains are diamond-shaped and the breaks are low triangles, inclined to them at 6°. The crown mains are pentagons abutting at the table and 18° steeper than these. As seen from above the cut gem bears a resemblance to an eight-petalled flower, though the number of 'petals' may be increased or decreased.

Star cuts may be exemplified by the *five-rayed star*. The gem is a pentagon in plan view. It has a table, but no culet, star facets, but no break facets, but the paired triangular facets converging at the point of the pavillion are described as *culet facets*. The angle of inclination of these facets to the horizontal is the *culet angle*. The mains are 9° steeper than this and extend halfway down from the girdle. As seen in plan from below the culet facets compose a five-pointed star. The crown consists of the conventional brilliant table, five mains and ten star facets interposed between them in pairs at 10° short of the crown angle in inclination. This cut is used for coloured stones of low to medium refractive index.

The *honeycomb cut* represents a marriage between the brilliant and the rose. As the name suggests, its mains are hexagonal. There are two rows of them, sixteen facets in each row, in both the pavillion and the crown, those near the girdle being the larger. Usually, if not inevitably, in the lower row of the pavillion mains, every second facet having a side in common with one of the eight culet facets is lopped off into a pentagon for cutting convenience (this is a matter of operational sequence). The culet facets themselves are likewise pentagonal and triangularly elongated towards the culet apex. The inclination increases towards the girdle by 7° with each successive row of facets, and the girdle (which is vertical as usual) is reached through sixteen triangular break facets at 20° off the culet angle. If we take the slope of the first (larger) mains in the crown as the standard of reference, the sixteen break facets at the girdle will be 7° steeper and the sixteen mains of the second row 7° less steep, while the sixteen star facets at the table are 15° (or 14°) short of the reference (crown) angle.

This somewhat intricate but attractive cut is suitable for stones of medium colour depth and low refractivity.

VARIATIONS ON THE STEP THEME

There are many other cut variants, based on the brilliant, step and rose patterns, including some asymmetrical ones, such as the obus, kite, shield, etc, which for reasons of space cannot be described in detail. We may, however, consider a concrete example of the emerald cut, used for such stones as beryl, topaz, quartz, apatite and fluorite.

Typically this is a three-step cut of eightfold symmetry. The gem is octagonal in plan view, and the octagon may be said to have been obtained by cutting off the corners of a rectangle, so that it has a pair of long and another pair of short straight sides at right angles to each other and four small oblique sides at the corners at 45° to either of the adjacent straight sides.

The crown part is quite straightforward, but there is some complication in the pavillion, which is cut deep in three steps, two of equal width and the third at the top, below the girdle, twice as wide as the others, all increasing upwards in slope by 10° with each step. There is no horizontal face at the culet, and the culet facets (the lowermost step) meet in a ridge. The break in the regularity of the pattern occurs on the short sides and at the corners of the solid. If we proceed down from the corners the two descending steps extend only as far as the culet facets, so that the first of them is a trapezium and the second a triangle. Down from a short side the first two steps are trapezia, but the culet face below which terminates the ridge is again a triangle. The width proportions and slopes remain unaffected.

In the crown all facets, except for the octagonal table, are trapezia decreasing upwards by 3:2:1 in width, and by 15° in inclination.

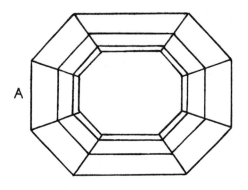

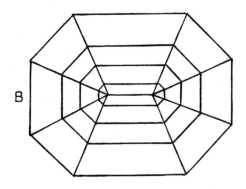

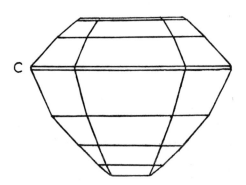

FIG 18 Example of step cut: A = crown (plan); B = pavillion (plan); C = side view

If we start from a square, instead of a rectangle, the culet ridge contracts into a point and all the four culet facets become triangles. Alternatively the design may be simplified in either case by making the short side and corner steps taper triangularly towards the culet ridge or point. This is the rule in the somewhat similar *bath tub cut*, which is twelve-sided in plan with two parallel long sides in the middle and five short sides of equal length at both ends of the 'tub'. By reducing the long sides to the same length as the short ones we obtain a *round step cut* of twelvefold symmetry, but the number of sides is inessential; it is, in fact, usually sixteen, having been derived from the traditional octagon. The number of steps can likewise be varied.

In the *single* and *double French stars* the gem is square in plan view and the crown and culet facets are triangular. In the *opposed bar cut* the crown is step-cut across the long axis of the gem. The number of steps is odd, with the highest step in the middle of the crown and two, three or more steps descending to the girdle symmetrically on both sides. The outline of the crown in plan narrows down stepwise concurrently with the transverse crown facets and terminates in a straight line along the last of these at each end, where the solid shape tapers down triangularly into the pavillion towards the culet ridge. Small break facets at the outside edge of the transverse crown facets serve to remove the sharp edge of the crown.

The simplest embodiment of the step idea is the *tablet cut*, which is a development of the table cut mentioned on p 58. Here the pavillion and the crown are mirror images of each other. Between the table and the girdle there may be two steps of trapezium facets or else triangular star and break facets of suitable inclination. Such a gem must inevitably be a 'fish-eye', except round the edges, where total reflection is possible. Consequently, this type of cut is suitable only for translucent (eg fire opal) or very dark stones (garnets, tourmalines, morions or amethysts of a very deep shade), but it may also be employed with minerals containing internal inclusions, eg rutilated quartz.

This survey is far from exhaustive, but should suffice to give a fair idea of the present state of the facetting art, as well as providing useful examples and suggestions to work from.

5

STONE INTO JEWEL

THE PROGRESS FROM THE ROUGH STONE TO THE POLISHED GEM MAY BE divided into five main stages: extraction; trimming to a suitable blank; grinding into shape or preforming; sanding; and polishing. Sometimes the raw material may take such a form, eg of loose, clear crystals, as to make extraction, or trimming as well, superfluous.

Extraction may be a hammer-and-chisel job. But such 'rough wooing' is not always possible or advisable, and sawing, slicing, or slabbing, may be necessary to divide a large mass into workable pieces, or to isolate the desired part of the raw specimen, say, a crystal or other inclusion from the matrix in which it is embedded, or the part of a large crystal selected for cutting. This may go no further than priming, an incision being made, into which a chisel is inserted to split the stone along the mark with a smart hammer blow. A refined version of this procedure is the bruting of a diamond, where the unwanted portions of a crystal are split off by utilising its natural cleavage (p 29). Indeed, the success of the technique depends on cleavage.

Splitting a stone along its natural cleavage planes may be easy, but attempting to do this in any other direction may end up in disaster. In any event this method requires a clear understanding of the properties of material and practical experience, and we would not recommend such treatment for crystals. Cautious priming and splitting may, however, be effective with amorphous materials devoid of cleavage, and small undercut or isolated pieces may be pulled off with pliers.

The priming can be executed with a diamond-charged file, and an ordinary steel file will do for materials up to grade five of Mohs' scale. A fine metal saw will cut, if somewhat laboriously, anything up to the same grade, and so can likewise be employed for priming. Theophilus in his famous *Treatise* described an ancient method of slicing a stone with a wood saw (there were no metal saws in his times), which was secured in direction by a pair of wooden pegs on both sides of the workpiece and moved back and forth (reciprocated) while sand and water were poured into the cut.

A later development of the same idea is to use a braided steel wire, which is either reciprocated or entrained in rotation by a pulley drive, with silicon carbide or other hard abrasive fed into the groove under the wire and lubricated with oil or water. This is a comparatively crude method of cutting a stone, which is done much more efficiently with a power-driven diamond saw but an amateur without one may do well to bear it in mind. It may also be used in the field on a collecting trip.

The trimming to a blank does not differ in principle from extraction, as both consist in removing unwanted parts of the workpiece; but in trimming, these parts are smaller and the margin of admissible error narrower.

The processes of cutting, grinding, sanding and polishing gemstones are all basically an extension of mineralogical scratch (p 13). Any mineral above another in the scale of hardness will scratch any one below it, and the more effectively the higher above it is. And it will be recalled here that making a scratch requires very little pressure. If too much pressure is applied the harder mineral can be crushed by a softer one, but this is not what we want. Gently does it, and too much 'vim' is good neither for the stone nor for the abrasive tool.

In nature diamond of grade ten will scratch any other mineral and is followed by corundum of grade nine, which is used as an abrasive in the coarse form of emery. Outside nature, boron nitride (BN), obtained by heating boron to white heat under high pressure in an atmosphere of ammonia, is harder than diamond, but at present is not commercially available as a graded abrasive. Boron carbide (B_4C), formed by reacting boron oxide with coke at 2,500°C, is another extremely tough material and has been used for charging abrasive tools, but so far not in lapidary work. Silicon carbide (SiC) or carbon silicide, commonly but incorrectly known as 'carborundum', is produced by fusing sand and carbon in an electric furnace, and stands at between $9\frac{1}{2}$ and $9\frac{3}{4}$ on Mohs' scale. Electrically fused alumina of cubic habit (and so unlike the hexagonal corundum of the same chemical composition, Al_2O_3) has a comparable hardness of 9·2–9·6. These two are common lapidary abrasives, good for anything short of diamond, which is traditionally ground and polished with diamond or bort grits and powders. Diamond powders may be produced artificially or by crushing poor-quality crystals and waste material from cutting. Bort, or boart, consists of radially crystallised black carbon granules of the same hardness.

DIAMOND ABRASIVES

GRADE	MICRON RANGE	USED FOR
40		Large saws
60		Preforming
80		Thin diamond saws
100		Rough (facet) cutting
120		Heavy (facet) cutting
230		Intermediate (facet) cutting
325		Medium facet cutting
400	30–60	Fine facetting
600	20–40	Rough finishing
800	15–30	Medium-fine finishing
1,200	8–22	Fine finishing
2,000	6–12	Extra-fine finishing
3,200	4–8	Rough polishing
8,000	1–5	Medium polishing
14,000	0–2	Fine polishing
50,000	0–1	Specialised super-polish

Lapidary abrasives are graded according to grain size by sieving, differential flotation or levigation, a process involving grinding to a fine powder in water and differential sedimentation, the heavier grains settling first. A grade is determined by the largest permissible grain size within it and marked by a number which denotes the number of openings per square inch in the sifting mesh: the higher the number, the finer the grain. Silicon carbide starts with grade sixty, which is comparable to sand, and goes up to 1,000, which is like fine flour. Diamond grits and powders span the grades from forty, used for charging large diamond saws and heavy-duty abrasive tools, to 64,000, where all particles are less than one micron, 1μ ($=$ 0·001mm), in diameter, employed for especially fine work.

Diamond and bort powders are much more expensive than other abrasives, but also more efficient and more durable, so that they may prove more economical in the long run. In addition they are usually ingrained in metal and so are not dissipated in the working.

This is so in abrasive tools (saws, files, drills), which all contain grains of hard material and operate on the scratch principle. They should, therefore, be applied lightly and not leaned upon in the same way as breaking and splitting implements that rely on mechanical action.

Extraction and trimming apart, the lapidary technique consists in grinding the stone into shape with coarser abrasives and then imparting to it a progressively smoother surface by reducing their particle size at each successive step. The highest powder grades are used for fine polish on facetted gems (see table above). The polishing operation, however, is not a matter of abrasion alone, and the smoothness of the surface may be at least partly due to the formation of the so-called Beilby layer, which is a fused film of molecular depth produced by frictional heat at contact between the stone and the polishing tool. This no longer depends on the hardness of the abrasive, and for this reason softer polishing agents may be preferable at this stage, as not all minerals respond equally well to diamond, bort or alumina. A Beilby layer, however, is not necessarily an advantage, as it has a tendency to recrystallise, yielding a matt finish and may have to be polished off to restore the brilliance.

In the past *rouge*, which is powdered haematite of grade six, used to be the favourite polishing substance, but it has lately fallen from grace, as it stains everything around it with red, and these stains are very difficult to remove (oxalic acid can be used on stones, but it is a poison and must be handled carefully). The same applies *a fortiori* to the green *chromium oxide* which is an excellent polisher. But, Glen and Martha Vargas in their book *Faceting for Amateurs*, recommend that 'it should be used only in desperation' when all else has failed. This is often the case with malachite. The white *tin oxide*, which is cheap, is free from this objection, as is the somewhat dearer yellowish-pink *cerium oxide* used for the beryl and quartz families of gemstones. *Tripoli*, a form of silica, has a cutting as well as polishing action and is sometimes employed in pre-polishing or improving difficult surfaces. *Putty powder*, too, is a possible polishing agent. Yet most of the polishing is done with some kind of alumina, such as *levigated alumina* or the American product marketed under the name of *Linde-A*. This is white, finely ground synthetic corundum, very accurately graded, and gives excellent results with most materials. It costs about ten times as much as cerium oxide, which tends to restrict its use to special occasions. On the other hand, like the diamond powders, very little of it is required to yield the same effect as a generous application of other polishing agents.

OF LAPS, WHEELS AND ABRASIVE HYGIENE

The abrasive or polishing powder is spread on, or worked into, some kind of support.

In the simplest case the support may be a piece of plate glass upon which the abrasive, mixed into a paste with oil or water, is evenly spread, the stone being moved by hand in a figure-of-eight fashion. This is not very difficult with softer materials, good preforms and finer powders; but cutting a hard stone to shape by this method takes a great deal of time and patience, and coarser grits tend to spit off the

73

glass in all directions. Still, it is true that quartz and even harder minerals can be dressed in this way. Rocking the stone and/or a small Pyrex bowl may be used to obtain a curved cabochon surface.

The polishing is done on a perspex plate, scored with a sharp knife or razor blade to hold the powder (eg cerium oxide), and a curved perspex surface, eg an old motor-cycle visor, may be similarly employed for cabochons. A felt or leather pad may be used instead of perspex.

Usually, however, the abrasive is carried by a revolving disc, against which the stone is held either by hand or by mechanical means. When the disc is mounted vertically and active at the rim it is spoken of as a *wheel*. Obviously, in this case the abrasive must be ingrained in the operative part of the disc, or else it would be flung off it by the centrifugal force of rotation. Indeed, in a *grinding wheel* (see plate, p 60), the abrasive, usually silicon carbide, is lightly bonded into a solid stone composition.

The *sanding disc* is a partial exception, inasmuch as a sheet of wet/dry silicon-carbide paper or the like of a suitable grade is exchangeably stuck to the flat side of the disc with a plastic, preferably non-hardening adhesive, and the workpiece is applied to the paper; thus, although a sanding disc is commonly mounted vertically and is therefore a wheel, it is inoperative at the rim.

Sanding discs, however, may also be mounted horizontally, and horizontal discs are generally known as *laps* (see plate, p 60), a description that again does not apply to sanding discs. Laps may be made of cast iron, copper, tin, lead, type metal, pewter, hardwood, such as teak or mahogany, sturdy plywood in the do-it-yourself version, plastic, leather, etc, depending on the type of work for which they are intended, and for very soft materials even of a mixture of beeswax and 10–15 per cent of carnauba wax supported on muslin and set in wood.

Bort or diamond powder is rolled into a copper lap with a copper roller. For the most part, however, the abrasive is applied to the lap when and as required in the form of paste, mixed with oil or water, usually with a soft water-colour brush from the inside outwards.

74

There are also manufactured pastes, especially devised to hold the abrasive. As an improvisation it is possible to use for this purpose odd pieces of lipstick, which though effective presents the disadvantage of strong colour. The mixture may be prepared in advance and pressed out of a plastic 'squeezy' bottle. Diamond powders of different grades can be bought in disposable syringes, which work on the same principle.

As laps revolve fast, it is an advantage to have them grooved or scored, to give additional purchase to the abrasive. The scoring may be radial or concentric. It may be obtained by using a 1in long segment from a hacksaw which has twenty-four teeth to an inch. Special scoring tools exist which impart concentric scoring to a revolving lap. Record discs, being already grooved, if pared down to an appropriate size and given a hard backing, make good polishing laps.

The polishing is done mostly on buffing laps or wheels (see plate, p 77), covered with leather, hard-packed felt or other fabric, which is charged with polishing powder. This is rubbed into the fabric with a little water. Excessive watering must be avoided for two reasons. For one thing it will inhibit the formation of a Beilby layer, which requires frictional heat, so that polishing action takes place mainly when the polishing paste is nearly dry, at least on the surface of contact with the stone. For another, wet fabric tends to rot and ruin the buff. In facetting, however, hard, slowly revolving laps, charged with diamond, bort or alumina powders are often preferred.

Clearly, the discs do not rotate by themselves and need some kind of impelling mechanism. This usually consists of an electric motor (a $\frac{1}{4}$HP one is adequate, though lower powers are used in commercial equipment), or at least of a treadle, shafts, journal bearings, a transmission gear, typically in the form of a driving belt with pulleys of different diameters for speed changes, guards, etc, which we shall consider in more detail later on.

It will be appreciated that, whereas the peripheral speed of a wheel is constant for a given number of revolutions of the driving motor and a given transmission ratio, the surface speed of a lap or a sanding

75

disc increases outwards from the centre in direct ratio to the distance from it, and so does the cutting or polishing action. This presents certain advantages, as the latter can be varied simply by moving the workpiece radially. On the other hand, if it were kept at a fixed distance from the centre in the same attitude it would be unevenly cut and to prevent this it must be rotated. Furthermore, to ensure a long working life and smooth action for either type of lapidary disc, it is necessary to keep the wear on its whole operative surface as constant as possible; otherwise it would become grooved and bumpy and need resurfacing, which can be done by means of a trimming tool, such as a razor blade with a stiff backing inclined against the sense of rotation. But this is a tricky operation and is better done on a lathe.

Another very important point may be described as *abrasive hygiene*. Once the stone has been roughly ground into shape, the whole process consists essentially in making progressively finer scratches on its surface until these become so fine that they can no longer be seen with the naked eye. This necessarily implies that all the coarser scratches from the foregoing working stage must be rubbed off in the next.

Thus if a single grain of coarser abrasive infiltrates the finer stage, not only will the effect be ruined, but the offending grain itself has to be located and weeded out. This can be done by testing the lap on a smooth face of a quartz crystal and marking the place where the coarser scratch appears. A magnifying glass will help, and the coarse grain will leave a tail of quartz powder behind it by which it can be traced.

In most cases, however, it will be easier to clean the whole lap thoroughly by washing, scraping with a razor blade as in resurfacing, or both. If all this fails the lap may have to be resurfaced on a lathe or even discarded altogether.

This makes it abundantly clear that any contamination of a finer by coarser abrasive must be prevented at all costs. The grits and powders must be kept separate, in tight, clearly labelled containers, such as cosmetic jars. Except for hard laps, which have to be scrupu-

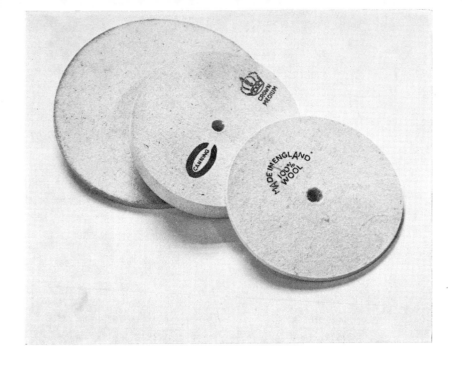

Page 77 (above) Felt (wool) polishing buffs; *(below)* Highland Park (American) Model E-2 trim saw for 8in or 10in blade, which has a cross-feed clamp (vice), slidable on a shaft, for holding the stone, an adjustable side support, or stop-guide, for accurate slicing, and a perspex guard among other features

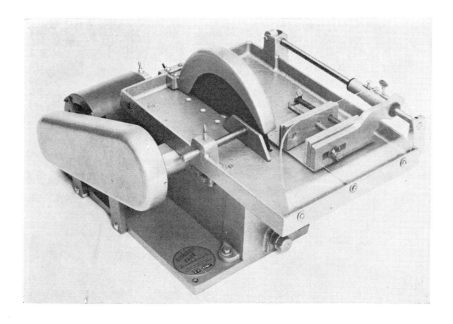

Page 78 (above) Using a trim saw. The stone is held between the thumb and forefinger (or two fingers) of both hands and fed gradually to the saw blade with even pressure. The stone must be kept flat on the saw bed; (below) Gem-Temp (Bitner) templates

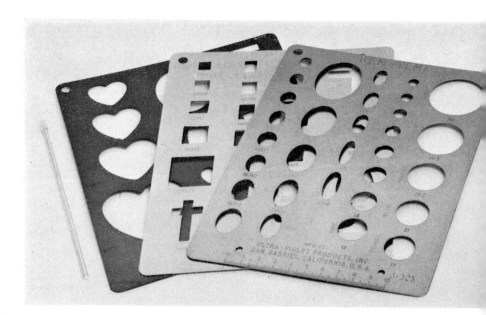

lously cleaned after use, abrasives of different grades or different abrasives of the same grade should never be used on the same lap. After every operation not only the stone itself, but the person of the operator, not forgetting the spaces under his or her fingernails, hair and clothes, must be conscientiously inspected and cleaned. The polishing laps and buffs, when not in use, may advantageously be protected by plastic covers (eg bags), as even ordinary dust often contains grains of sand that could prove fatal in the polishing. For the same reason the workroom should be kept as free from all dust as possible.

DIAMOND SAWS

Whether our material be found or purchased, we will generally have a piece of stone or rock that is still too large after such trimming as can effectively be done with hammer and chisel without wasting good stuff. This is where a diamond saw comes in.

The operative part of the machine is a disc, or blade, of mild steel or phosphor bronze, charged at the rim with diamond grit. The thickness of the blade varies from $\frac{1}{16}$ in to $\frac{1}{8}$ in according to the diameter, which ranges from 4in to 36in, or their metric equivalents. The large saws are called slabbing saws, as their main use is for cutting large stones or pieces of rock into slabs, and the smaller and thinner ones —trim or trimming saws, and sometimes slitting saws, terms that are self-explanatory.

For reasons that will become apparent later on, the blade is thickest at the rim, where it has an inward taper. The diamond charge may be sintered into the rim all along it, in which case the saw can be run either way, and will, in fact, benefit by an occasional reversal of the sense of rotation. In a notched blade, however, the diamond-metal sinter is distributed in notches or segments along the rim, and such blades have a fixed sense of rotation, which is specified in the manufacturer's instructions.

In an ordinary amateur workshop there will not be much scope for a heavy-duty 36in saw, and a combination of a 10in slabbing

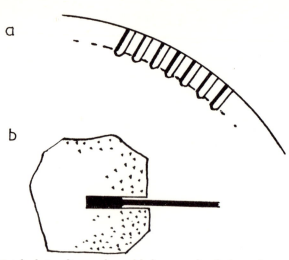

FIG 19 Notched rim diamond saw blade: *a* = detail; *b* = clearance
made by blade in sawing; note right-angle engagement of
stone by blade

and a 4in trimming saw will be adequate, while a 6in or 8in saw
may do for both types of work.

The blade is usually mounted vertically, running towards the
operator in an enclosed tank holding a suitable lubricant-cum-
coolant, provided with a splash-guard and driven by an electric
motor over a V-belt and pulley transmission. The coolant, which acts
also as a lubricant, should be of low viscosity, not readily in-
flammable or vapourisable, and if possible odourless. It is questionable whether the traditional mixture of oil and paraffin answers
these requirements. Texaco 519 and Castrol Syntilo 303 oils, the
latter of which is water-soluble and usually diluted in the proportion
of 70:1, are often recommended. One of their advantages is that
the rock flour produced in the sawing tends to settle at the bottom
of the tank with clear oil above. For sawing porous materials and
turquoise and opals in particular, oils are unsuitable and pure water
should be used instead.

The tank must be periodically inspected, cleaned when fouled,

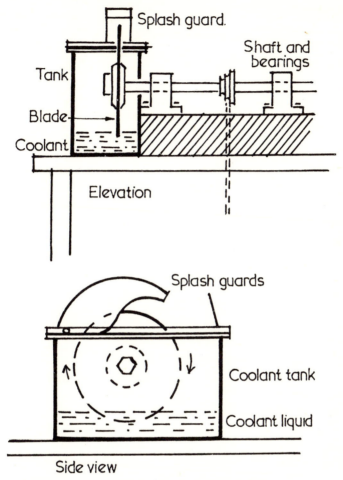

FIG 20 Sectional views of a 'home workshop' diamond saw,
mounted on workbench. Motor can be fixed either below or
behind the shaft

and refilled. To prevent overheating, the level of the lubricant should
not be allowed to drop too low, but immersion of about half-an-inch
will be adequate for a small saw.

The saw works very much like a circular timber saw, but on the

81

principle of mineralogical scratch. The blade will not injure the hand if touched lightly, even when revolving at high speed, which is usually some 2,000 surface ft per min, corresponding to over 1,200 revolutions in a 6in blade, though opinions as to the preferred speeds differ. Even in ordinary sawing it is important to keep the saw straight and apply it at right angles to the surface to be cut, and this is all the more so here, as the speed of rotation is high and the thin blade can easily become buckled (it is also expensive—£5 ($12) or more).

The blade must be cutting over its whole depth (see Fig 19). If the stone is not held quite straight throughout the sawing operation there will be more pressure on one side than on the other, and the blade will be worn down unevenly to a V-edge, so that the cut becomes too narrow for the body of the blade to follow and it jams. This is why diamond saws usually widen out at the rim.

All this necessitates very accurate guiding. It is helpful to mark the line of the cut, for instance, with an aluminium pencil. This can be purchased from lapidary outfitters, but practically any sharp aluminium point will do. The stone is then brought up very gently against the edge of the revolving blade, which is kept on the marked line as the cutting proceeds. With hand feed, it is recommended to support the stone on both sides with the thumb and two fingers (index and middle) (see plate, p 78). The feed, however, may be automatic, with the stone held between the jaws of a clamping device, which presents it to the blade, and the pressure of application adjustable by means of weights on a wire.

If the stone is too small or too awkwardly shaped for accurate guiding and square presentation, it may become necessary to mount it on a block of wood with dopping wax (see p 86) or even in a block of cement, which is then handled as a unit and on which the cutting lines are drawn. For this purpose some lapidarists use a mixture of white cement with vermiculite, in which the stone is suitably embedded, placed in a paper-lined box and left for four days to allow the cement to set. A fifty-fifty mixture of a cellulose filler and ordinary cement serve equally well and set within a day.

In any kind of sawing the tricky moment arrives when the saw is about to break through, and this is when damage to the rapidly revolving blade is to be feared. It is advisable to reduce pressure and if the saw can be stopped without letting go of the stone (eg in the case of mechanical feed or if there is a companion who can switch off the motor) to withdraw the stone and break the remaining bridge by hand. Brittle, splintery materials, such as obsidian, crystal aggregates in the cores of agates and some metallic ores, are also unhealthy to diamond saws and must be handled with great care. The blade must always be kept clear of loose chips.

It is further necessary to guard the blade against over-heating, which is bad for blade and workpiece alike (the latter may crack under thermal strain). For one thing an adequate supply of clean coolant must be ensured. Should overheating threaten, the pressure must be reduced, and, if possible, the operation interrupted, to allow the blade to cool, and the speed reduced.

Yet, however carefully a diamond blade may be handled, a time will come when it grows dull and loses its bite. This is due to the diamond particles having been driven into the metal and bridged over. Reversible-drive blades can be improved by making them turn in the opposite sense; notched blades cannot. The saw has to be cleaned up, which can be done by running it through a soft sand brick. The suitability of the brick can be tested by turning the bit of a screwdriver in its surface: if the screwdriver scoops up brick dust easily it is all right.

Large slabbing saws serve primarily to cut large massive stones into slabs of suitable thickness, which can then be divided into smaller blanks. A trimming saw is used for the latter operation, as well as for trimming the blanks.

Cutting crystalline material is a more delicate operation, and where cleavage is well developed the cuts are made, if possible, along the cleavage planes.

6

THE FORKING
OF THE WAY

TRIMMING FOR A CABOCHON

A DIAMOND SAW WILL BE REQUIRED IN ALMOST EVERY CASE. BUT THE
cutting of loose crystals involves only the removal of the unwanted
parts to isolate the future gem. This will usually be facetted, which
massive material seldom is, although there are no hard and fast rules
here. Our procedure, however, will vary depending on whether we
are cutting a cabochon or a facetted gem. The working stages are
basically the same, but there are important differences in the techniques and machines employed in the two cases.

A cabochon can be cut on a lap, which may be provided with
special grooves for this purpose, but this type of lapidary disc
serves primarily for cutting flat surfaces. On the other hand, while
it is not impossible to produce facets on a vertical disc, and appropriate appliances have been devised for this, such an arrangement
necessitates charged discs, and conventional facetting machines
operate horizontally. Thus, although some of the teaching relating
to cabochons is equally applicable to facet cutting, the two procedures
are sufficiently different to require separate consideration.

The end of the foregoing chapter has left us with a flat slab of stone,
which is the usual prelude to a cabochon. We may further assume
that the slab has been cut into blanks of sizes appropriate for the
intended products, and one of these blanks has now to be trimmed
to the required outline.

This outline must be clearly and carefully marked, say, with an
aluminium pencil, or *scriber*, for which purpose use may be made of

a *Bitner template.* A Bitner template (see plate, p 78) is a sheet of transparent plastic (perspex) with apertures of graded shapes and sizes, corresponding to the conventional cabochon types (rounds, ovals, teardrops, hearts, squares, crosses, etc), which saves a lot of trouble, especially to those who are not good at drawing. If, though, we are bent on a polygonal or some other unusual shape, we have to work this out for ourselves, first on a piece of paper and then transfer it on to the stone blank.

Whichever the case may be, the parts of the blank beyond the mark have to be eliminated. This can be done with a trim saw, especially if straight lines are involved in the design, or by grinding, which will largely depend on how much surplus material there is.

A saw cut must always be made at right angles to the edge. A blank will generally have a more or less irregularly curved edge, along which points suitable for square sawing can be found. The usual procedure in trimming a blank is nibbling or notching its edge with a saw, which will result in a number of salients. For obvious reasons the notches or nibbles will have a tendency to converge, so that the salients will taper inwards and can often be broken off with pliers. This opens up the possibility of approaching the remaining salients at right angles from the side, in which case they can be sawn off. Indeed, if the outline comprises straight lines the notching must be so manipulated as to make straight cuts possible at the right places. We must, however, keep an eye open for the structural properties of the stone, such as cleavage and twinning planes, or layering in concretional material (eg agates), which may develop into lines of weakness. If these are disregarded the blank can easily be spoiled.

For a similar reason the notches should stop short of the marked outline. In case of doubt it is safer to grind away the unwanted portions on a *grinding wheel,* which will have to be used for accurate trimming in any case, unless we employ a diamond file instead. On softer grades of stone an ordinary steel file or even sandpaper can be quite effective, however much the 'pukka' lapidarists may frown on such crude methods.

Sharp points are unhealthy to grinding wheels, and since a few such will probably arise in the notching or nibbling, it may be advantageous to smooth them down with a file before the grinding. Failing this and remembering the mineralogical scratch principle, which continues to apply, the rough-trimmed blank should be brought into contact with the wheel very gently, although the pressure of application may be increased once the jags have gone.

A large blank may be held in the hand during the preliminary grinding. But some stones will be too small to do this conveniently, or effectively, and will have to be dopped.

DOPPING

The object of the *dop, dopping stick* or *dopstick*, is to provide a handle at the end of which the stone can be firmly but removably mounted, so that its sides can be readily exposed to the grinding, cutting or polishing action. In cutting a cabochon the stone should be easily rotatable. For this reason the dopstick is usually round, either a piece of wooden dowel or a similar metal (aluminium) rod, some 4in to 5in long. Metal dops often have a depression at the end, which makes it easier to hold the bead of wax, cement or resin upon which the stone is mounted. The rear end is rounded, so as not to cut into the palm of the hand in which it is held; the dops used in facetting machines may have a pointed rear end.

The diameter of the stick will vary according to the size of the stone it carries. It must be sufficiently thick to give the stone a firm purchase, but leave it projecting on all sides for easy access. An assortment of dopsticks of likely diameters will be required.

Sealing wax is quite adequate for mounting the stone. Alternatively button shellac may be used, or sealing wax with a scale of shellac under the stone. Special dopping cement can be bought from dealers or made according to the following recipe: sealing wax 4oz, shellac $\frac{1}{2}$oz, plaster of paris $\frac{1}{4}$oz, powdered resin $\frac{1}{4}$oz; heat and mix thoroughly.

Heat-sensitive stones, however, such as opals, may preferably be dopped by a cold method. A proven way is to mix a little corn-flour into dough with clear acetone adhesive, mould the dough on the dopstick into a support, put a touch of adhesive on the stone, press it into contact and mould the dough round its base, to make it firm. This dopping mixture disintegrates in acetone.

Cellulose acetate, used for model aeroplanes, can be mixed with cornflour or starch in a similar way. The product marketed under the name of 'Glyptal' or 'Stronghold Cement', soluble in acetone or methyl-ethyl ketone, is also suitable. Catalyst-hardening polyester resins have sometimes been used, but cannot be recommended. They are very strong, but take a long time to set and are difficult to remove, which can be done with solvents sold for epoxy glues. Some lapidary outfitters supply cold-dopping cements which have been developed in diamond sawing. These do not dissolve in oils, but are slowly soluble in water, though they will withstand a light trickle of water used for lubrication without excessive softening. Alternatively shellac can be mixed into a thick paste with methylated spirit, which evaporates fairly rapidly. The shellac hardens to a horn-like con-sistency, but remains soluble in spirits.

The general disadvantage of cold dopping is that the cement requires a lengthy period to harden, so that the stone cannot be worked immediately as with dopping wax. The wax is fixed to the end of the stick when hot and reheated to plastic condition for setting the stone, which must be clean, free from oil or moisture, and is itself heated to the approximate temperature of the wax.

There are various ways of doing this, but the following method has been found particularly effective. The wax is heated in a shallow tin (lid) over a low flame (spirit lamp, gas ring, bunsen burner or the like) until it flows freely. The wax is not allowed to boil and bubble, however, for this would reduce its plasticity and make it hard and brittle. A simple method of avoiding overheating is to place a spirit lamp, which consists of a broad vial filled with methylated spirit and a wick, inserted into it through a suitable stopper with a mechanism (a small toothed wheel) for raising and lowering the wick, to control the height and so the heat of the flame, within a

87

strip of sheet metal bent into a U shape and mounted on stone or an asbestos plate (see Fig 21). The top limb of the U then acts as a hot plate, on which our tin of wax is placed for heating.

When the wax has reached the right consistency the dopstick is dipped into it about half-an-inch deep, promptly withdrawn and put vertically head down on to a cold smooth surface, which may

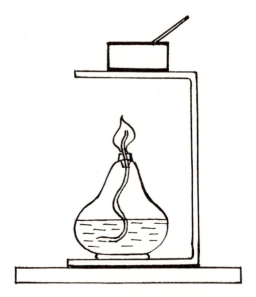

FIG 21 U-shaped metal strip as support and hot plate. Heat to dopping wax in a dish is supplied by a small spirit lamp

be wetted to prevent adhesion. This will produce a cone of wax at the tip of the stick, which is now ready for further use. Several sticks of different dimensions, thus prepared, may be suitably stored; for instance, stuck vertically with wax uppermost in a piece of cardboard with appropriate holes placed over a box or tin, or a block of wood with vertical bores.

When the time comes to dop the stone, both it and the wax on the stick must be heated, but not to the original temperature, as all that is required is to make the wax plastic and mouldable and the stone sufficiently hot so as not to chill the wax on contact. The correct temperature of the stone may be gauged by placing upon it a flake of, or a pinch of powdered, shellac: when this begins to melt the stone is ready. A brief heating on the hot plate should suffice for that, but, unless a cold dopping method is used, stones sensitive to heat should be warmed up slowly in a shallow tin filled with sand.

We now turn the stick upwards, press the stone firmly into the base of the wax cone, and then mould the wax underneath it with moist fingers into a bevel which leaves the rim of the stone free. The wax must be allowed to set and cool, which does not take more than a few minutes.

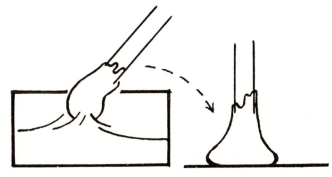

FIG 22 Preparing a dopstick

As the grinding, sanding or polishing proceeds, the dopped stone has to be inspected from time to time. It must be guarded against overheating for the twin reasons of losing its footing in the wax and thermal stresses. It has to be washed for inspection, which again involves a similar hazard. If cold water were poured over a hot stone the rapid chilling could cause it to contract and jump out of its seat, in addition to the risk of its cracking under the strain. To prevent this, the water may be heated to the approximate temperature of the stone; or else the stone be allowed to cool.

Eventually the time will come when the job is done and the stone must be removed from the dop. Sometimes a gentle knock may suffice to dislodge it. Alternatively putting the stone under a cold tap may do the trick, with the reservations just mentioned in the preceding paragraph. It may, however, be safer and altogether more satisfactory to effect the release of the stone by placing the dopstick, cooled down to room temperature, in a refrigerator. If this fails, or for any other reasons of convenience, the stone may be reheated until the wax softens and then pulled off the dop. The effect is not so neat, and some wax may be expected to be left adhering to the stone. With stones of grade six or harder, this can safely be scraped off with a penknife, and whatever remains washed off with methylated spirit or carbon tetrachloride, which dissolve both conventional dopping wax and shellac. Acetone or special solvents have to be used with plastic cements.

GRINDING INTO SHAPE

Thus our stone has been roughly trimmed and dopped, and is ready to be ground into shape.

A lapidary grinding wheel is not unlike the kind used to sharpen cutlery, though it may be ruined if so employed. It operates on the same principle, but the difference lies in that it is made with carefully graded, soft-bonded silicon carbide, ensuring uniform grinding action and giving the wheel a porous, water-pervious texture, which prevents its becoming glazed in use, as an ordinary wheel would be. Silicon carbide grits are available in grades from 60 to 600, and even finer, loose, on paper, or cloth. But in most lapidary machines there are only two wheels: one of grade 80, 100 or 120, and another of 220 for finer working. They may be exchangeable or mounted in pairs on the opposite sides of the same driving shaft for equilibrium, made to turn towards the operator under a splash guard and lubricated with a trickle of water, which drips off into a sump underneath the wheel.

Like the laps, the wheels should be used uniformly over the whole grinding surface, to prevent their becoming 'dished', grooved or bumpy. Should this happen, however, the pristine condition can be

restored by pressing a *diamond wheel dresser* against the perimeter of the
rotating wheel, to scrape off the damaged surface. This will also
remove any glazing that may have developed.

Six-inch grindstones, 1–1½in thick, are deemed adequate for an
amateur workshop. Rim grinding speeds may vary from double the

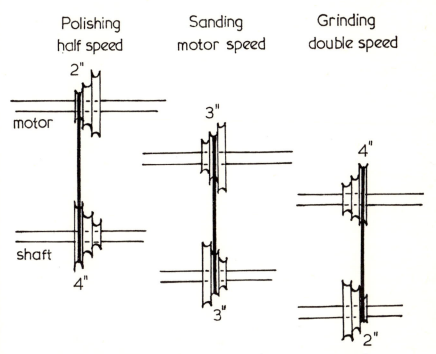

| Polishing | Sanding | Grinding |
| half speed | motor speed | double speed |

FIG 23 Stepped pulley system. 2–3–4in combinations in reversed
order on driving and driven shaft yield half motor speed,
motor speed and double motor speed, for polishing, sanding
and grinding respectively

motor speed for coarse grinding and preforming to motor speed for
the finer wheel. Most British ¼HP motors run at 1,425 revolutions
per minute (rpm), and American motors are quoted at 1,725rpm,
but other powers are also used, which serves to complicate matters.
Speed changes from half to double motor speed are achieved by a

three-step pulley system (2in, 3in and 4in) on shaft and motor. Speeds may be given in rpm or sfm (surface feet per minute). To convert the former into the latter, the circumference of the wheel ($2\pi r$, $2r = \frac{1}{2}$ft in our case) must be expressed in feet and multiplied into rpm and the transmission ratio.

The manufacturers usually specify the maximum permissible speed for their wheels. Lower speeds increase the wear on the wheel; higher speeds are used with wheels of harder bond (less porous), which tend to glaze and require frequent dressing. The coarse wheel wears down about twice as fast as the fine.

The base of a simple cabochon may but need not be polished, that of a double or hollow cabochon must be. In every case it is normally cut first and bevelled round the edge, to prevent chipping and facilitate mounting, while the blank is trimmed to the marked outline, undopped (see plate, p 95). But small stones may have to be dopped with the bottom part uppermost first and then reversed, even in cutting a simple cabochon (see plate, p 95). It is, therefore, on the bottom part that the outline is marked. In the case of stones of uniform colour and texture it may not matter which side of the blank is top or bottom, but if there are marked differences in colour and pattern, as in most agates, or flaws to be concealed, some thought must be given to the final effect at the outset.

To simplify matters, let us consider a simple cabochon.

It has been assumed so far that the stone has the form of a slab or slice, sawn off from a larger block, but this need not be so: it could be a rounded pebble or a chip, which has first to be ground to a plane surface on a lap or the side of a coarse grinding wheel. In either case we will end up with some kind of solid having one large flat face that extends approximately to half its depth and is laterally bounded by a more or less regular, typically oval, outline.

A half-pebble thus obtained is already domed to some extent, and so approximates to a cabochon shape, which may simplify the grinding operation. A chip may be so shaped as to suggest a teardrop or angular outline, and it saves a lot of trouble to follow nature as far as possible. In such cases the distinction between trimming to a marked outline and grinding into shape, or preforming, is some-what blurred. In fact, there may not be much point in marking an outline at all; it may be better to dispense with punctilio and trust the eye and the hand to turn out a pleasing form.

Regardless of these varied possibilities, and of whether the stone be dopped or not during the trimming stage, it is generally presented to the wheel in such a way as to prevent sharp edges digging into the

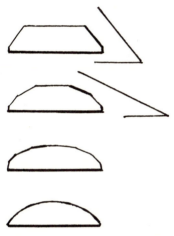

FIG 24 Shaping a cabochon dome. Progressive stages, from top to bottom, changing angles of cut

grinding surface, both to conserve this surface and to avoid the stone getting caught and jerked by the revolving wheel. The stone is trailed across it, preferably against the sense of rotation, with the crown forward.

The trimmed stone is dopped on its flat base in the way described in the preceding section. First its sides and then the top of the crown, which must be accurately located, are ground to shape on the coarse wheel (see plate, p 95), and the preform thus obtained is finished off on the fine wheel. The object of the next processing stage is not so much to improve the shape of the stone as to remove the crude

93

scratches left by the grinding. It is described as sanding, although it may be carried out with loose or ingrained abrasives on a lap or a small grooved wooden wheel (eg of maple or tropical hardwood), charged with diamond powder.

In the case of a double cabochon the bottom, or pavillion, part has to be processed in full before the stone is redopped, substantially as in facetting (see Chapter 9). The same is true of a hollow cabochon, whose concave pavillion cannot be cut on a grinding wheel or smoothed on a sander, and requires a small button lap with a convex surface.

Cutting a ball or ellipsoidal bead involves an extension of the double-cabochon technique, and the stone has to be redopped several times, to obtain a perfectly smooth round surface. In fact, special machines exist for cutting balls. There are also semi-automatic cabochon machines whose operation is controlled by cams guided by a template. Few amateurs, however, will need or be able to afford such refinements, which, in any case, are more suited to mass production than to the enjoyment of a hobby.

SANDING

The further processing calls for finer abrasives. The essence of the procedure lies in first removing the coarse scratches left by the grinding and then progressively scratching the surface to a dull 'satin' finish, sufficiently smooth to accept final polish. The stone must be carefully cleaned and examined through a magnifying glass at the end of each stage. Should any coarser marks have survived from a preceding stage, the stone must be reworked before moving on to the next stage, because deep scratches become more and more difficult to remove as the size of the abrasive grain decreases. This is especially true of the polishing stage, where abrasive action is very small, so that deep scratches only tend to be emphasised by the surrounding polish. For this reason the intermediate stage of sanding is extremely important, and spending a little time on it may save many a tear later on.

94

Page 95 (*above*) A cabochon blank being trimmed (undopped) to the marked outline on the grinding wheel; (*below*) shaping the cabochon dome on a grinding wheel. The stone must be kept moving, to prevent formation of flat facets and points. Note position of the hands, holding the dopstick, supported near the wax and rotated at the end by the right hand

Page 96 (*above*) A cabochon being cut on a lap. Grinding and sanding can be done on such machines; (*below*) sanding a cabochon on a 220 wet/dry sanding disc. Water is supplied from a squeezy bottle

Strict abrasive hygiene is obviously a must. Laps coated with a slurry of loose abrasive will serve, but complicate the hygiene problem. The standard method is to use a *sanding wheel* (see plate, p 96), or other sanding apparatus, which is usually incorporated in a combination machine.

The sanding wheel consists of an aluminium or sturdy plywood disc, some 6in across and ⅛in thick, coated on one side with semi-hard rubber (this yields to some extent to a curved surface), which is fixed to the disc with Evo-stik (a plastic glue) or similar adhesive. A sheet of tracing cloth is superimposed (sized face outwards) on the rubber as a bearing surface for a disc of silicon-carbide paper or cloth of the wet-dry type, removably attached with a non-hardening adhesive (eg 'Tacky Adhesive'), such as is used in self-seal envelopes or on sticky tapes. The disc is usually mounted vertically and rotated at motor speed. Papers or cloths of grades 220, 320 (400) and 500 (600) are successively used; and, since the grit gets worn down as well as the stone, a well-used 400 paper will give as fine a finish as a new 600 one. In fact, some materials respond better to an old paper.

A paper disc wears down faster at the edge than nearer the centre, and can be revived by washing and brushing from inside outwards, which removes the clogging stone dust. An old worn-down paper can be reconstituted by coating it thinly with water-glass and sprinkling with the grit of the right grade, the surplus of which can be shaken off by turning the recoated paper upside down. Cloths are more durable than papers, and lately diamond cloths and papers have appeared on the market. These are more efficient and last even longer, but are also much more expensive than the silicon-carbide ones. Another variation on the same theme are plastic discs with ingrained abrasive.

Belt and drum sanders are alternative forms of the same device. In the belt sander, the cloth or paper web is carried like a conveyor belt over two rotary rollers. In the drum version there is only one large roller, or drum, and the sanding paper is stretched over it in the form of a sleeve. The advantage of these designs is that the whole of the operative surface is readily accessible and moves at the same speed, which ensures uniform cutting action, whereas a wheel is much more effective near the edge and practically useless in the middle. On the other hand, the cutting speed cannot be varied so easily as it can on a sanding wheel by simply moving the workpiece to and fro.

A sander can be worked dry, especially at a low speed, but the process generates a lot of dust as well as heat, so that the wheel or belt is usually washed and cooled with a jet of water from a fine pipe placed above it, or, failing this, from a clean 'squeezy' bottle. Low speed, insufficient watering and excess of pressure may give rise to undercutting, the sander tearing out small particles from the surface of the stone, and the 'orange skin' effect, to which some agates, containing sugary quartz aggregates, are particularly prone. If there are any flat facets, eg on an agate slice with rounded edges, excess of pressure against the rubber-mounted sanding paper, which yields to it to some extent, may result in a dull centre. Such a facet may have to be resanded with coarser abrasive or even reground before it can be successfully polished. 'Pre-polishing' with Tripoli powder may help.

POLISHING

The polishing, which is the final stage of working a stone and has been discussed on pp 75 ff, is done at about half the sanding, and so motor, speed, though lower speeds are used with diamond powders. The stone must be very carefully cleaned and examined for scratches, but if the sanding has been well done the polishing does not present any special difficulty. The stone, however, becomes strongly heated during the polishing, which may cause it to crack or even fuse on the surface, so great caution is advisable.

As mentioned on pp 73 ff, the sanding and polishing operations can be carried out manually, without machinery. Softer materials can be effectively sanded dry on ordinary sandpaper, and harder grades on emery or carborundum paper or cloth. The polishing is then done on scored perspex, felt or leather with cerium oxide or like abrasive mixed with water.

Such methods are, of course, relatively slow and inefficient, but they are worth mentioning for the sake of an amateur who does not want to invest in complicated equipment. They may also allow of a greater degree of control, and sometimes produce better results than power-driven machinery, especially with difficult materials.

As already indicated, the gloss on a polished gem is due partly to the scratches being so fine as to be invisible without sufficiently high magnification, and partly to the formation of a Beilby layer. The effect varies according to the material and the polishing agent. No Beilby layer forms on diamond, nor is it produced when diamond powders are used for polishing. The same is largely true of other hard powders.

The absence of a Beilby layer necessitates very small grain size. In fine diamond powders it is below 1μ (p 71); Linde-A is graded down to 0.3μ, and Linde-B to 0.05μ. Silicon carbide is not available in grades over 1,000, which corresponds to a micron range of about 10–20 and so is unsuitable for fine polish. Thus, apart from Tripoli, other polishing agents rely mainly on Beilby.

The latter is due to frictional heat, so that such polishers require higher speeds than the hard abrasive type. In polishing with diamond the speed need not be high, and in modern cabochon machinery diamond powders of grades as high as 50,000 or even 100,000, supplied in syringes and applied with an extender fluid, are worked into small, fat wooden wheels, $1\frac{1}{2}$–2in deep and 3–4in across, with a partly concave 'dished' perimeter. The wheels are made of some close-grained hardwood. Maple, lignum vitae, yew are commonly used for this purpose. Tropical hardwoods without clear rings of annual growth are particularly suitable. A concave polishing surface in the form of a broad groove at the edge of a lap (p 84) will be found useful for cabochon work in any case.

The dual nature of polishing action is the main cause of the unequal response of different materials, and even of different samples of the same material, to a given combination of lap and polishing agent. Generally speaking, the harder the mineral the harder will also be the most suitable lap and powder. Diamond is polished with

99

diamond on cast iron, corundum on copper or zinc, apatite and fluorite require a lead or type-metal lap, but the much harder tourmaline too responds to this treatment, while quartz and beryl gems are often polished on laps made of 'Lucite', a variety of hard acrylic plastic.

The behaviour of both minerals and powders is sometimes capricious and unpredictable. Glenn and Martha Vargas record in *Faceting for Amateurs* (pp 222–3) that one batch of cerium oxide gave good results with agates and chalcedonic silica in general, but not with quartz, while another batch of seemingly identical powder was quite satisfactory with quartz as well. If one combination does not work, the only way is to try another.

Most polishing agents are lubricated with water, but if water is hard it is advisable to add a pinch of detergent; in fact, a little detergent will never hurt. Herbert Scarfe has found that a few drops of acetic or oxalic acid may improve the polishing action in difficult cases. Diamond powders, however, are traditionally mixed with paraffin, and no water is used on wooden polishing wheels charged with diamond; the stone may be worked dry at low speed or periodically dipped in olive oil, always with the due reservation for porous, absorbent materials, and turquoise in particular, where oils must be avoided and water used instead.

It is a mistake to apply too much powder to a buff or lap; a well-worked one that seems visually devoid of polishing powder will usually perform just as well. Finally, it will do no harm to repeat that in polishing the same lap should never be used with different polishing agents.

All of this applies to cabochons and facetted gems alike.

A well-polished surface should show no scratches under a linear magnification of five to ten times. Another test is to place the stone under the head of a strong electric bulb and examine the reflection. If the inscription on the bulb can be read from it (under magnification on a convex cabochon surface) the stone is declared well and truly polished.

7

FACETTING

PREPARATORY MOVES

FACETTING INVOLVES TECHNIQUES AND CONSIDERATIONS NOT EN-
countered in cutting cabochons. The initial steps of trimming and
grinding to preform are common to both, except that facets are
typically cut on transparent, crystalline material, which will not
generally have the form of slabs or slices. Sanders are not used in
facetting, the facets being cut to progressively finer finish on graded
laps. Moreover, since a facetted gem has to be worked to equally fine
finish both top and bottom, or crown and pavillion, either the one
or the other must be taken to the final polishing stage before the
stone can be reversely dopped in accurate central alignment for
working the other half. This is a tricky and important operation,
which will be given full attention later on.

The cutting of a double cabochon, a ball or a hollow cabochon
presents a similar problem, but with rounded surfaces the risk of
serious misalignment is far less severe.

Additional points that require attention in facetting are cleavage
and optical properties, already touched upon in the earlier chapters.
Amorphous materials or crystals with undeveloped cleavage are
comparatively easy to handle, but where cleavage is present the
facets of the gem must be, if possible, so oriented as to miss the
cleavage planes by at least 10°; otherwise they will tend to chip in
the cutting and wear. This is particularly true of the table, which is
the largest single facet. For instance, topaz splits very easily at right
angles to the long axis of the prism, so that the table must intersect
this axis at not more than 80°. This done, we need not worry about
cleavage so far as the remaining facets are concerned. Some minerals,

however, cleave in two, three or more directions, and are correspondingly more difficult to deal with. The cut has to be very carefully planned. The table given below will be of some assistance here. While it is comparatively easy to determine the cleavage planes in a shapely (euhedral) crystal, crystals are often compound, twinned or otherwise involved, so that their local cleavage planes may be at variance with the general plan and have to be unscrambled. In ill-defined chips or water-worn specimens the situation is complicated by the lack of clear bearings. If the material is pleochroic or birefringent its crystal axes of symmetry and hence cleavage planes can be deduced from its optical behaviour. Another pointer is small fractures, which will be smooth and shiny along the cleavage planes.

BRITTLE AND CLEAVABLE GEMSTONES

NAME	WHETHER BRITTLE	CLEAVAGE
Actinolite	yes	Good, often lamellar, 1 direction
Anatase	no	Perfect, 2 directions
Andalusite	yes	Poorly developed, 1 direction
Apatite	yes	Absent
Axinite	yes	Fairly distinct, 2 directions
Azurite	no	Good, 1 direction
Beryl	yes	Absent
Brookite	yes	Poorly developed
Calcite	no	Perfect, rhombohedral, 3 directions
Cassiterite	yes	Partial
Cordierite	no	Poor, 2 directions
Corundum	yes	Absent, but plate crystals common
Diamond	no	Perfect, octahedral, 4 directions
Diopside	no	Distinct, often lamellar, 1 direction
Dioptase	no	Good, 1 direction
Epidote	yes	Perfect, 1 direction
Felspar	no	Strong in 1 direction, weak in other 2
Fluorite	no	Perfect, octahedral, 4 directions

NAME	WHETHER BRITTLE	CLEAVAGE
Glaucophane	no	Perfect, prismatic
Idocrase	yes	Absent
Jadeite	yes	Prismatic, 2 directions
Kyanite	no	Very strong, partial, 2 directions
Lapis lazuli	no	Variable, 6 directions
Lazulite	yes	Absent
Malachite	no	Variable, sometimes good
Marcasite	yes	Very poor
Natrolite	no	Perfect, 2 directions
Nepheline	no	Distinct, 1 direction
Prehnite	yes	Distinct
Pyrite	no	Variable, sometimes good
Rhodocrosite	yes	Very strong, 3 directions
Rhodonite	no	Perfect, prismatic, 2 directions
Rutile	yes	Poor, 2 directions
Scheelite	yes	Variable, 2 directions
Sillimanite	no	Perfect, 1 direction
Sodalite	no	Poor according to *Dana's Manual of Mineralogy* (see p 205); distinct, 6 directions according to some other authorities
Sphalerite	no	Perfect, 6 directions
Sphene	no	Fairly distinct, prismatic, sometimes lamellar
Spodumene	no	Well developed, 2 directions
Topaz	no	Perfect, 1 direction
Tourmaline	yes	Absent
Zoisite	no	Perfect, 2 directions

As previously indicated (p 69), cleavage may be utilised in trimming, but is troublesome in cutting. Unidirectional cleavage, exemplified by topaz and epidote, does not present a serious problem. But minerals with prismatic or four-directional cleavage (along planes parallel to crystal faces), such as diamond and fluorite, require careful mapping before the cut is made. Calcite and sphalerite are not normally reckoned among gems in view of their low hardness (3 and $3\frac{1}{2}$ respectively), but have sometimes been cut to good effect; they are also troublesome.

Brittle minerals must obviously be handled with care: the general rule is to reduce pressure and speed, and avoid overheating.

Some of the most difficult minerals are relatively soft and opaque, and in facetting opaque or translucent materials optical considerations can be left aside, except inasmuch as schiller, adularescence or opalescence may be involved. In transparent gems, however, optical effect is basic.

PLANNING THE OPTICS OF A CUT

Optical staff work begins with ascertaining the presence and location of flaws.

The simplest and most effective way of doing this is immersing the stone in a liquid of identical or closely comparable refractive index, which, bar colour differences, makes the stone more or less invisible and its internal flaws stand out. Ideally an assortment of liquids could be contrived exactly to fit every required refractive index. This, however, is not really necessary. Moreover, some of such liquids, and those of high RIs in particular, are troublesome—poisonous or subject to discolouration upon exposure to light. Two or three liquids may suffice in practice. Carbon disulphide (CS_2) with RI 1·64 is good enough for stones of RI up to 1·85, but has an unpleasant pungent smell and is subject to rapid evaporation. This need not be too serious if it is kept in a tightly closed jar with a ground stopper, a spring clip or a screw-on cap holding down a glass lid against a rubber ring, or the like. But acetylene tetrabromide of RI 1·63 is almost equally effective and free from these objections. It can be used for anything from quartz to demantoid (see table, p 46). Cinammon oil (soluble in alcohol) has an RI of 1·59 and is suitable for the range from fluorite to topaz. The commercial product

'Refractol' (RI 1·56), soluble in acetone, is comparable. But ordinary water-soluble glycerine (RI 1·47) is almost as good and covers the minerals from fluorite to beryl. Refractive indices can be reduced by adding a graded quantity of solvent.

The liquids, if kept in the suggested way, are virtually immune to evaporation and will last for years. The immersed stone is usually held in self-locking tongs.

If the flaw is a bad one the corresponding part of the stone will have to be cut off, often taking with it a large portion of the clear material. With minor flaws, however, it is often possible so to manipulate the cut as to conceal the flaw under one of the break facets near the girdle, where it is least noticeable.

Contrariwise, if we want to emphasise a blob of strong colour, such as often occurs at the base of an amethyst crystal, or some interesting inclusion, the cut is so arranged as to place it centrally just above the culet point, where it catches most of the reflected light and is itself multiplied by reflection from the pavillion facets. For instance, a quartz crystal may contain a needle of tourmaline or rutile *flèches d'amour*, and it may be possible so to design a brilliant-type cut that the needle comes to stand up vertically from the culet point towards the centre of the table. It will then be multiplied by reflection and refraction into a symmetrical kaleidoscopic pattern. The effect in a step cut is not equally striking, but will depend on the number and arrangement of the inclusions and facets. Where the inclusions are very numerous it is usual to have recourse to the table or a tablet cut, to show these to the best advantage. Alternatively they may be brought into the girdle plane of a fully facetted gem, which is also the place for a strong coloured layer that is to be emphasised.

As mentioned on p 39, the colour in tourmaline, cordierite and some other minerals depends on the direction of viewing, and the cut has to be planned for the desired effect.

The table acts like the object glass in a camera or a telescope: it serves for gathering light, the inclination of the pavillion and crown facets being such as to ensure that most of the light thus gathered experiences total reflection from the former and can pass out again through the latter. On the other hand, the table appears dark when seen from the side under vertical illumination, which is reflected toward the viewer by the crown facets. The combination of the two is meant to give the gem the maximum attainable sparkle in every

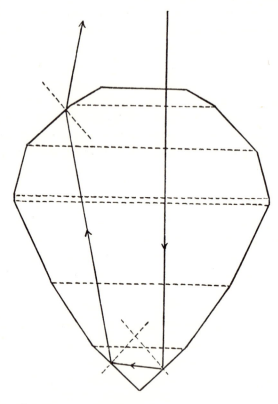

FIG 25 Path of a vertical ray of light in a step-cut quartz gem

position, and the compromise is achieved by giving an equal share of the gem's cross section to both; in other words, the table in the standard brilliant and most other cuts occupies half the width of the gem. This rule, however, is not inviolable, and especially where the emphasis is on colour the table may be somewhat larger (this makes the gem appear larger as well, but the objection that this is, therefore, 'dishonest' cannot be taken seriously).

Another approximate rule, likewise derived from the practice of diamond cutting, is that the pavillion should be twice as deep as the crown. This is sound enough on the average, but in cutting coloured stones a deeper cut is used with the paler and a shallower with the darker ones. Since such stones are more often than not cut in step, there will usually be more steps in the pavillion of a pale gem.

Our freedom of choice, however, is restricted by the necessity of obtaining total internal reflection from the pavillion facets of a ray vertically entering the table. For this purpose the ray must strike the facet at more than the critical angle (the angle of incidence and/or of refraction is measured from the normal at the point of incidence), its angle of incidence being equal to the angle between the facet and the plane of the girdle. If the pavillion, especially culet, facets are made too steep a point will be reached where the vertical ray reflected from a facet on the one side of the pavillion will strike the corresponding facet on its opposite side at less than the critical angle and so be refracted out of the gem, instead of being returned through the crown. The best results are obtained with the pavillion mains angled to the girdle plane at the gem's critical angle plus 2 or 3°. The break facets (at the girdle) are 2° steeper.

The behaviour of light in a cut gem can be studied vicariously on paper with pencil, ruler and protractor. For this purpose we draw a cross section of the gem through the centre of the culet, the centre of the table, and in the brilliant or the cuts derived from it—through the centre of the pavillion and crown mains (see Fig 25). Any ray vertically incident upon the table passes on unrefracted; the angle of incidence is equal to the angle of reflection; and where refraction occurs the angle of refraction can be found, knowing the RI, from mathematical tables (see p 191).

However, if the reader is insufficiently numerate for these calculations it is not really necessary to know the precise angle of refraction, which will always be larger than the angle of incidence on the way from stone to air and *vice versa*. The only thing that matters is whether the ray within the stone is incident at an angle below or above the critical. In the latter case it will be reflected back into the stone, which is advantageous in a pavillion, but wrong for a crown facet. This much can be ascertained by making an accurate geometrical drawing, without any reference to mathematical tables.

It is thus possible to check up how sound our cutting plan is, and to improve it if necessary. Fig 12 shows the optimal arrangement for a standard quartz brilliant. In a step, or emerald, cut (p 66), the situation is more complicated, but the principle is the same. The cutting angles given in Chapter 5 will be satisfactory for gemstones with critical angles between 38° and 41°, but may require revision for higher RIs.

FACETTING MACHINES

Facetting is traditionally done on rotary horizontal laps of various materials and abrasive grades, according to the nature of the operation and of the stone. There exist vibratory laps, which cut a flat facet by a circular oscillation of small amplitude, instead of rotation. Vibration, however, is undesirable in facetting, as it tends to produce dull edges, so that such laps are not used in facetting machines, where interchangeable cutting and polishing discs, about 6in (15cm) in diameter, are mounted upon a rotary platform or turntable, usually set upon a well-balanced vertical shaft, in a shallow splash-tray. The shaft is driven by an electric motor. The suitable speeds and powers are a somewhat controversial issue; $\frac{1}{4}$HP or $\frac{1}{6}$HP motors and speeds of 300rpm or more are commonly used, but some experienced lapidarists recommend powers as low as $\frac{1}{10}$ HP or $\frac{1}{20}$ HP, and much lower polishing speeds. Speeds of 100rpm with tin or lead laps are suitable for materials such as apatite, axinite, diopside, idocrase, kyanite, etc, but may be as low as 35rpm with wax laps used for soft minerals, eg calcite or sulphur, should you wish to try your hand at these. The general rule is that soft, and/or brittle, and/or easily cleavable materials are worked on soft laps at low speeds.

V-belt and pulley transmission is usual, as in the machinery described in Chapter 5, but continuous electronic speed control with friction coupling presents manifold advantages, although it is more expensive.

There is nothing in the nature of things, apart from skill and labour, to prevent a stone being facetted by hand without special machinery. The table is often polished by hand anyway. The chief difficulty derives from the fact that the stone may have to be reset on the dop-stick for every facet. The simplest way to ensure the correct angle of

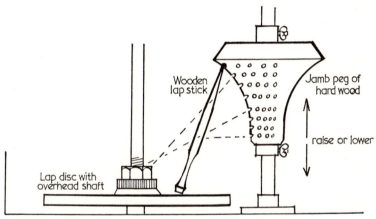

Wooden lap stick

Jamb peg of hard wood

raise or lower

Lap disc with overhead shaft

FIG 26 Jamb peg machine. Facet angles and indexing controlled by inserting lap sticks into appropriate holes in the jamb. Traditional lap sticks (or dop sticks) made of hardwood 5–6in long, with pointed ends

cut is to dop the stone so as to make the facet lie parallel to the cutting surface when the stick is held vertically at right angles to it. The accuracy of such work must necessarily be low, and success with anything more complicated than a single-step table cut is problematic.

The problem consists in keeping the workpiece fixed at the correct inclination in the vertical plane and in the correct angular position relatively to the axis of the dop (indexing). It should also be possible to move the workpiece up and down the lap, which serves to control wear and cutting speed (p 76).

This problem can be solved in a number of ways. The oldest solution, still widely used in some professional establishments in Germany and Israel, is the *jamb-peg machine* (Fig 26). In this a plate or a pear-shaped body, made of hardwood or other suitable material, with a number of inclined holes bored in it for the reception of the dopstick, is traversably mounted on a jamb projecting over the lap. The inclination of the holes corresponds to that of the various facets, the correct settings being obtained by moving the dopstick from hole to hole. No provision is made for accurate indexing: the dopstick is simply turned round in its hole for cutting the successive facets.

FIG 27 Milling exercise piece

The easiest way is to cut the opposite parallel facets first, then the pair at right angles to these, and finally interpose the intervening $45°$ facets, to complete an octagon. Simple aids to correct positioning can, however, be readily contrived: eg passing the dopstick through a six- or eight-sided nut.

If a *milling exercise* piece (Fig 27) is adapted for a cutting head we have an exactly opposite situation, inasmuch as it ensures accurate indexing, but leaves the matter of inclination open. A milling exercise piece is a conically convergent piece of metal, cut, or milled, into a number of equilateral polygonal plates, starting with a triangle at the thin end, progressively increasing in diameter and number of sides, and terminating in a circle at the broad end. Making such a piece is a standard exercise for factory apprentices, and, though not commercially available, it can be obtained on request. All that is needed to convert it into a *facetting head* is to drill an accurately centred bore through the long axis of the piece for the insertion of the dopstick. Some provision must be made for immobilising the stick in the bore, eg by passing it through a sleeve (tube), technically known as the *quill*, which is rigidly fixed within the bore, and securing it there by means of a grub screw. Alternatively the grub screw may be in a collar fixed at the rear end of the piece.

To operate the head, it is further necessary to have a horizontal bar, plane-parallel to the lap and mounted upon a vertical *stand rod*, or *mast*, alongside it. The successive facets are cut by supporting the head upon the bar on the sides of the requisite polygon (octagon, hexagon, etc) and turning the polygon round. The inclination is varied by raising or lowering the bar upon the mast, where it can be secured at various heights. The corresponding angle can be measured with a protractor.

O'Brien's machine (see plate, p 114) is an application of the same idea, except that the indexing polygonal plates are separate and exchangeable.

In most modern machines, however, the facetting head comprises a quill, holding the dopstick and adapted for stepwise rotation by means of a toothed wheel and a trigger catch. The angular position of the dopstick is fixed for each facet by this *indexing mechanism*. The number of teeth in the wheel is usually made divisible by three and eight, which allows the most popular gem cuts to be indexed. The indexing, however, may also be effected by means of a micrometric screw and angular scale with a grub screw.

The quill is secured to a support, which is either itself movable along a graduated arc or pivots on an arm projecting from the mast against a protractor, which is usually a quadrant marked from o to 90°, and where a pointer, perpendicular to the quill and so parallel to the girdle of the stone at the end of the dopstick, shows the inclination of the facet which is being cut. The protractor scale may be equipped with a vernier for greater setting accuracy. There will also be an *angle stop* to immobilise the quill relatively to the scale.

The horizontal arm carrying the head can be moved up and down the mast by means of a supporting collar-and-screw, rack-and-pinion or worm-and-nut arrangement and secured at the desired height, while left free to turn horizontally (see plate, p 113). It is

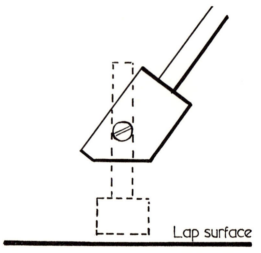

FIG 28 Forty-five degree adaptor. Position of dopstick shown in interrupted lines. Used for cutting and polishing crown table

further useful for the arm to be hingedly articulated in such a way as to allow the quill to be raised for inspecting the work done on the facet. The mast itself is horizontally slidable along a line passing through the axis of the shaft driving the lap and immobilisable at any desired distance from it.

It is thus possible to cut a facet at any angle from $0°$ to $90°$ to the girdle. But the cutting of the table may present certain difficulties, which can be overcome by using a $45°$ *dop*. This is a metal block, shaped like a brick with one edge bevelled at $45°$ and pierced by a vertical bore for holding the dopstick. The bevelled edge is adapted

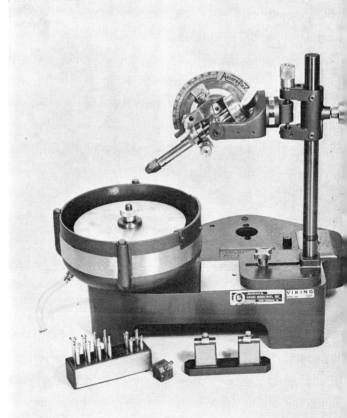

Page 113 (above) Ezycut (Australian) Little Jewel Facetting Machine. Left: lap assembly with splash pan and master lap, large pulley for speed reduction. Centre: Stand rod (mast) with facetting head, including a protractor quadrant for setting angles and a notched indexing wheel. Height of facetting head is set by supporting collar-and-screw. The stand rod is longitudinally slidable in a slot in machine base. Right: electric motor bolted in position; (right) Viking (American) Accuraflex Facetting Unit. An example of a highly sophisticated machine. A set of dopsticks, 45° dop and transfer jig are in the foreground.

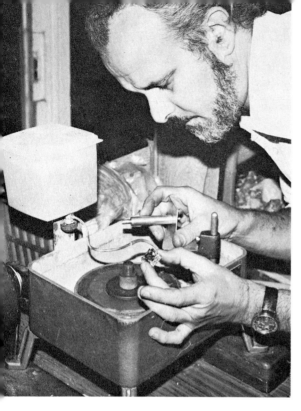

Page 114 (above) 'Gem Master' machine (see p 140) by M. L. Beach, of Twickenham, England, makes use of O'Brien templates; (right) Geogem (British) facetting appliance, comprising a sophisticated head on a mast, swivellable upon a stand. Transfer jig and a set of dopsticks in foreground

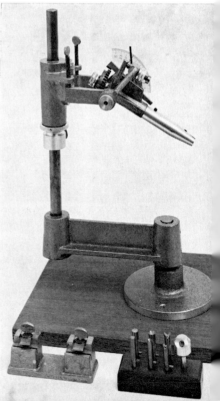

to be fitted to the quill or dop chuck, so that when the latter is in the 45° position (pointer central upon the protractor scale) the dopstick will be perpendicular to the lap.

DO IT YOURSELF

There is a wide range of fine lapidary machines of all kinds awaiting the customer, and the prices are not all that high: photographic cameras can cost more. Yet in the days of increasing dependence on vast industrial combines and impersonal organisations there is a growing desire to shake ourselves free from all that and rely on our own resources. This is largely what hobbies are all about.

Constructing a complex modern photographic camera may be beyond the effective reach of an amateur. But from the engineering standpoint a facetting machine is a comparatively simple piece of equipment, which can be built from odds and ends, perhaps with some assistance, unlikely to be refused, from a garage, a bicycle repair shop, or a local locksmith (if there is one to be found). In a school, a well-equipped metal-working class will have all the necessary tools; but if we go as far as that we might as well have a complete engineering workshop. Many lapidary clubs and individual enthusiasts have succeeded in this venture at very modest expense with little more than a file, a vice and a metal saw. It can be done, all the more easily as many lapidary outfitters stock shafts, pulleys and other vital machine parts (see plate, p 131), which can be acquired relatively cheaply, thus simplifying the job of construction. Alternatively or concurrently, such parts can be obtained by 'cannibalising' discarded items of household gadgets: washing machines, vacuum cleaners, bicycles, etc.

The job falls into two parts: facetting lap and facetting head.

A facetting lap is only a special case of the lapping machine and can indeed be used as such without a head. The work it has to do is comparatively light. On the other hand, it has to be very steady and free from vibration for accurate cutting. Facetting laps can take various forms (see plates, pp 113, 114 and 131), but typically we have a

revolving disc, master lap or turntable for the reception of exchangeable cutting and polishing laps, mounted upon a vertical shaft, spindle
or arbor, which is held in some suitable bearings and driven by an
electric motor through a V-belt and pulley transmission. The part
of the shaft above the turntable is usually of a reduced diameter and
threaded for securing the exchangeable laps by means of a nut. The
turntable is surrounded by a shallow dish or tray, known as *splash
tray*, for catching and holding the stone debris and such lubricant
as there may be. In lapping machines provisions are made for the
supply of lubricant or coolant by means of a *drip feed* and for waste
disposal. In a facetting lap, however, there is comparatively little
waste and special arrangements may be dispensed with, although the
tray will require cleaning, so that at least a waste pipe may come in
handy. On the other hand, the rim of the splash tray must be sufficiently low to allow for cutting girdle facets at right angles to the dop,
which then lies very close and parallel to the lap face. The problem
can be solved by reducing the height of the rim on the side facing
the head and covering up the gap with a removable segment of sheet
metal or plastic (see p 131, lower plate).

It should not be too difficult to come by a disc suitable for the
turntable. A cooking plate from an old electric cooker has been
known to be utilised for this purpose, and a sprocket wheel from an
old bike could be similarly adapted. In the latter case the pedal shaft
may also make a good arbor, the more so as it is already provided
with ball bearings and *races* (ie tracks in which the balls run).
Alternatively, for instance, a 'Picador' sealed shaft with ball-race
bearings can be purchased from a hardware store.

Whatever we do, the important point to bear in mind is that the
turntable must be mounted true upon the shaft (arbor), ie lie at right
angles to its axis over the entire surface of the table, and run without
any wobble, whether vertical or horizontal, to cut a perfect facet.
For this reason the turntable should not be mounted straight upon
the shaft, but rest upon a broad collar or a spider (a collar with
flat-topped prongs, usually three), screwed or brazed on to it. It is
of advantage to have both the turntable and the shaft relatively

massive, which increases their rotational stability and makes them less susceptible to vibration. Other things being equal, it is also of advantage to have as short a shaft as possible. Often there is a very short, thick arbor journalled between the turntable on the one side and the pulley on the other. But a short arbor may not allow enough room for a triple pulley, of which the 'Picador' type mentioned above is an example, and it is advantageous for smooth running to have the shaft journalled on both sides of the pulley, where it is exposed to a disturbing side force.

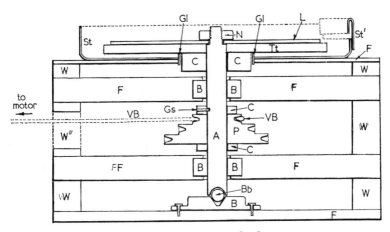

FIG 29 Example of lapping machine suitable for facetting in section. Background parts not in section in interrupted outline: A = arbor with reduced part at top end and cup-like recess at bottom end for reception of ball-bearing Bb; B = bearings; C = collars; F = frame; Gl = gland; Gs = grub screw; L = lap; N = nut retaining L; P = pulleys; St = splash tray; St' = part of St of reduced height with removable guard; Tt = turntable; Vb = V-belt; W = wooden blocks spacing metal parts of frame F; W' = opening in W for Vb

Thus the construction illustrated in Fig 29 may be worth a little extra trouble. Here the arbor is journalled on both sides of a triple pulley in bearing blocks with bushes (see plate, p 131), although some other type of bearing could be used as well, and rests at the bottom end upon a single large ball bearing fitting into a cup-like recess fashioned in the end of the arbor on the one side, and into a conical recess in a pillow block screwed to the frame on the other. The pulley is secured to the arbor by a grub (headless) screw in the central member and supported by collars on both sides. The collars may be fixed in position by three equispaced screws fitting into hollows in the arbor (shaft.)

The pulley is driven by an electric motor (not shown) through a V-belt, which can be moved into any of the three grooves on the pulley and the corresponding pulley on the motor shaft (Fig 23). It will be recalled that the transmission ratio is the ratio of the radii (or diameters) of the input (motor) and the output (arbor) pulley. If the latter is, say, 4in and the former 1in across, the motor speed will be reduced to one-quarter, and pro rata. The motor must be adjustably mounted, to allow for the changing length of the belt between it and the lap arbor.

A $\frac{1}{4}$HP motor may be obtained from an old washing machine. Vacuum cleaners are another potential source of motors, and a kitchen mixer can provide a low-power, though rather noisy, motor. Electric drills are not too expensive and have low-power motors that can be utilised for our purpose. All that is needed is to clamp a snub axle with a small pulley in the drill's chuck, which, incidentally, does not preclude the use of the drill for its normal or other purposes (eg for driving a small profiled wooden wheel for cabochon work). The drill should be rigidly mounted, preferably not on the machine frame itself to reduce vibration. If an electronic speed reducer is employed speed reductions down to 25rpm (which is unlikely to be required) become possible.

The machine illustrated in Fig 29 affords no more than an example of possible construction. It can be greatly simplified, having only a single massive bearing below the turntable and only one pulley, which may be exchangeable, below the bearing. This may be adequate for facetting and polishing, while the illustrated construction can be used as a general-purpose lapping machine, beside providing increased stability, important for accurate facet work, without greatly increased outlay, or labour. We can thus, as it were, 'kill two stones with one lap'!

Such a machine should make proper provisions for lubrication and cooling, which cannot come amiss in any case. A splash tray may be improvised from a baking tray or a plastic bowl with the sides cut down to the required height, pierced to receive the arbor or the collar holding the turntable, which should be protected by a gland, or surrounding ring, against contamination by grinding slurry. The lubricant-coolant may be applied as and when needed from a 'squeezy' bottle, but it presents no special difficulty to acquire a plastic bottle of suitable size and provide it with a drip feed (plastic tubing) and a cock. There should also be an outlet with a waste pipe leading to a sump (any odd tank or pail) for waste removal.

All this cannot be left suspended in the air and requires a suitable frame of solid construction. Large Meccano-type perforated metal strips of assorted lengths, angle brackets, matching bolts and screws are commercially available and can be used to construct the skeleton of the casing, but are not massive enough by themselves to be vibration-proof. They may, however, be fitted into or over a wooden framework, or else wooden blocks may be used as spacers. Again old machinery can be cannibalised for construction.

The bearings must be very accurately and firmly mounted. Ideally special metal castings would have to be made for this, which may be difficult without adequate equipment. On the other hand, fibre-glass, 'plastic metal' and various plastic cements can be moulded cold, set very hard and bond to metal. A provision should be made for lubricating movable parts (oil hole). Bearing bushes impregnated with graphite do not require lubrication.

FACETTING HEAD

A factory-made precision facetting head may cost £50 ($120) or more, but is an even easier do-it-yourself proposition than a lapping machine.

A milling exercise head described on pp 110 ff is one possibility. A jamb-peg or an O'Brien head is quite easy to make, but even the proper mast-cum-arm with protractor scale and indexer presents no insuperable difficulty.

Again there are many possible variants, but I would suggest the

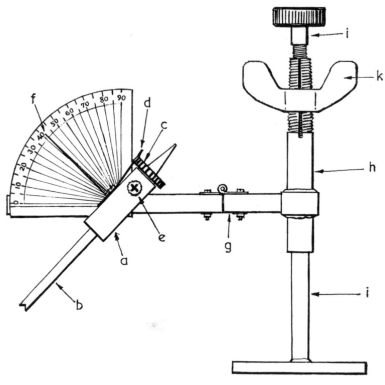

FIG 30 Facetting head and mast suggested in the text (pp 117 ff). Side elevation: a = quill (dop holder); b = dopstick; c = notched indexing disc; d = spring clip; e = screw with knurled or milled head for securing the dopstick; f = protractor quadrant and pointer; g = hinged arm for the head; h = sleeve holding g and slidable upon mast i; i = mast; j = part-threaded bolt with milled head for controlling the height of h; k = winged nut for clamping j

following arrangement, partly illustrated in Figs 30 and 31, if only by way of example.

First we have the mast, which must be brazed, screwed, or otherwise rigidly secured to a massive strip of metal, adapted to slide immobilisably upon a firm base plate fixed to the machine frame. It is suggested that the mast be a smooth vertical rod, over which a sleeve carrying the arm for the head is slidingly fitted. The top part of the sleeve has an inner screw-thread, which may be countersunk, for the reception of a bolt, matchingly threaded in its upper portion, but smooth and of reduced diameter in its lower part. It may have a milled or polygonal head (Fig 30). The height of the arm upon the mast is controlled by screwing the bolt in and out. To prevent the bolt from slipping, the topmost part of the sleeve may be given a slight conical taper, two diametrically opposite slots, and a short length of outside thread adapted to receive a winged nut, as shown in the drawing; or an outwardly milled or otherwise roughened and inwardly threaded ring, in such a way that when screwed on, it compresses the slots and secures the bolt in position.

The arm, which is simply a rectangular metal bar and could be improvised from a spanner, is solidly united with the sleeve, eg by brazing. It may advantageously be cut in two, fairly close to the mast and reconnected by a top hinge, so that it can be lifted for inspecting the progress of the work on the stone, but will resume the horizontal attitude under its own weight. The quill holding the dopstick is a sturdy metal block with a central longitudinal bore for the dopstick, which can be secured in it by means of a screw (Figs 30 and 31). The quill is made to pivot upon the arm, and has a pointer extending at right angles to it from the pivot and sweeping a protractor quadrant, fixed to the arm. There is a further screw, passing through the arm and a slide-block, or spacer (Fig 31), for immobilising the quill in the desired angular position. The end of this screw and its track upon the slide-face of the quill may be roughened up for better engagement.

In order not to complicate matters, the dopsticks, which are relatively cheap, may be purchased. Indexing presents no great

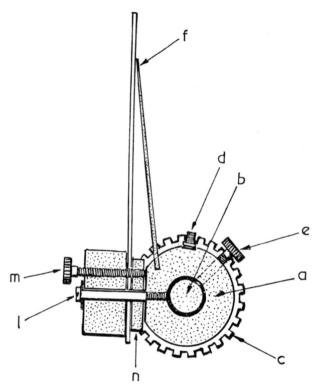

FIG 31 Facetting head set at 90° seen head-on in partial section along
the pivot (metal parts in section stippled): l = pivot; m =
flat-end screw with milled head for securing the quill in
indexed position (the end of the screw and its track on the
slide face of a may be roughened up to improve purchase);
n = circular block. Other designations unchanged as in
Fig 30

difficulty either. It should be easy enough to obtain a pinion having
a required number of teeth (24, being divisible by 4, 6 and 8, is a
useful number). Alternatively a regular polygon or a notched disc
can be cut and filed from a suitable piece of metal (brass or aluminium may be easier to handle than steel), and a hole drilled through
the middle of this, through which the tail of the dopstick is passed.

Both may be made square, to prevent rotation. The trigger catch is simply a leaf spring, engaging the gaps between the teeth of the pinion, the notches or the flat sides of the polygon, which may be notched in the middle for accurate positioning. No great force is needed here, as the indexing template is in rigid engagement with the dopstick, which is itself secured in the quill by the screw. Exchangeable indexing templates with different divisions may be provided for cutting gems with different numbers of sides.

Various modifications of this scheme are possible.

8

STEP BY STEP
TO A FACETTED GEM

TRIMMING AND PREFORMING

AS STATED IN THE PRECEDING CHAPTER, THE TRIMMING AND PREFORM-
ing, or grinding, stages are common to the cutting of cabochons and
facetted gems. But a facetted gem requires far greater accuracy and
elaboration, which is reflected in every processing stage.

An ordinary general-purpose diamond (p 80) may be used
for trimming crystals, but the cut is comparatively wide and correspondingly wasteful if the crystal is small and precious. To
eliminate waste, use may be made of a very fine *facetter's trim saw*, with
a blade only ten or twelve thousandths of an inch thick. Such blades
are very fragile, and must be handled with utmost care. Accurate
guiding and square presentation are vital. If the crystal is to be cut
at an angle it must be mounted in cement (p 82), on which the line
of the cut is marked with an aluminium pencil. Otherwise the lines
are drawn on the crystal itself. A waterproof felt point pen may be
used instead of an aluminium pencil.

The trim lines follow the outline of the intended preform as
closely as possible, but with a safe margin, to absorb any possible
errors and to allow for the material to be removed in the subsequent
grinding.

If a small flaw is present the cut is made on the outside of it, but
through the middle of a large flaw, where possible, so as to save good
clear material on its either side for future use. It will also be recalled
that trimming cuts are made in line with the cleavage planes.

Sawn stone surfaces have a mat 'frosted' finish, which obscures internal flaws, but these will show clearly if the stone is immersed in a suitable liquid (p 104) or even water, or if the surface is varnished.

The position of the cut gem in the rough must be planned well in advance, and if the material is to be used economically, advantage must be taken of the geometry of the crystal. Prismatic crystals are usually at their clearest at the tip, and when this is pyramidal it makes a natural approach to the shape of a pavillion. If a prism is step-cut lengthwise, then again its sides provide natural edges for the gem. Thus, unless cleavage or flaws intervene, it is often possible to work quite close to the crystal shape.

In simple brilliant cuts the gem is about three-quarters as deep as it is wide and the pavillion is twice as deep as the crown, but multifacet types of brilliant require greater depth, and in step cuts the width and depth are about equal. If, however, colour effects are involved the depth may be increased for pale stones and reduced for dark ones. For most minerals the inclination of the crown and pavillion mains alike to the girdle plane is 45°. But in multifacet brilliants and step cuts an allowance has to be made for the additional facets between the culet and the girdle, which results in a preform that is somewhat wider than required for a simple brilliant.

As mentioned earlier, the (crown) table usually extends to a half of the gem's width, but may be somewhat smaller in step cuts. It is not generally an advantage to have a flat culet, but if the angles are to be maintained and the stone is cut shallow it may be necessary to have a horizontal facet at the culet.

It is well to bear all this in mind already during the trimming, to avoid later adjustments and waste of material.

Grinding to preform may be carried out on a grinding wheel, as in the case of cabochons, or on a coarse lap. For this purpose the trimmed stone is mounted on a wooden dopstick with the ordinary dopping wax or cement. Since both crown and pavillion have to be preformed, the stone will have to be reversed on the dop, and at this stage it is better to work the crown first, as the accurate positioning of a pointed, or at least concurrent, pavillion on a wooden dop is difficult.

It is usual to grind 'round' and 'oval' brilliants, etc first into cylinders of corresponding outline, and then bevel these in rough correspondence with the envisaged facetting. This procedure, however, may be wasteful in the case of regular crystals which have natural faces that lend themselves to developing into a cut shape (see plate, p 131). For instance, beryl often occurs in very accurately hexagonal columns, and if the gem is arranged with its vertical axis coinciding with the long axis of the prism there are obvious advantages in basing the cut on the hexagon, rather than forcing the standard octagon on the hexagonal crystal.

In cutting a standard brilliant the simplest way is to grind both ends of our cylinder into 90° cones (45° angle at the base), and then slice off a half of the crown cone, which yields the correct proportions.

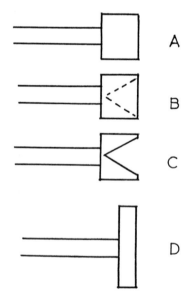

FIG 32 Facetting dopsticks: a = flat dop for securing table; b = hollow conical dop for round brilliant pavillion; c = V-shaped dop for step-cut pavillion; d = face-plate, used for accurate alignment

Special devices exist that ensure correct preforming of the more complicated patterns, such as ovals, marquises, pendeloques, etc.

THE FACETTING PROCEDURE

Our preform is now ready for further processing, and here utmost accuracy is vital, for if a single facet is out of place or at a wrong angle the whole scheme is upset, and the resulting errors may be very difficult to correct.

Facetting dopsticks are made of metal, usually aluminium, and, since they have to fit a standard quill or chuck, they all have a shank of the same thickness, but different heads (Fig 32). Some will be wider, others narrower than the shank. They may end up as a flat disc, a triangular channel for step cuts, or a conical depression to receive the pavillion of a round gem. In view of this a much wider assortment of dops is needed for facetting than for cabochon work.

The first move is to transfer the stone from the preforming to the facetting dop. All traces of wax must be removed from the preform by scraping (the scraping tool must be softer than the stone and applied gently) and washing in methylated spirit or carbon tetrachloride—alternatively, acetone or like solvent in cold dopping. Since facetting necessitates great working precision, stronger and less fusible dopping material (a melting point of 150–180°C, or 300–350°F) is used. On the other hand, many crystals are heat-sensitive and must be protected against rapid changes of temperature.

The stone is heated gradually, eg in a sand tray, as suggested on p 89, or else small dabs of molten wax are applied to it, to raise its temperature, and only the dopstick is exposed to direct heat. A good plan is to coat the stone with liquid shellac and allow it to dry. This creates a good bond between the stone and the wax and greatly reduces the need for heat. Facetting wax is mainly shellac in any case. Cold cements make such precautions unnecessary, but are troublesome in other ways, especially in redopping.

To ensure accurate alignment, use may be made of a *preform holding plate*, which is simply a thick metal plate with triangular channels and conical recesses, to accommodate rectangular step and round brilliant preforms respectively. Once the pavillion rests flush in one of these recesses, the table of the preform will lie horizontally, which should yield an accurate dopping when the dopstick is brought to bear against it centrally and vertically from above. A still better alignment can be achieved by using a *redopping* or *dop-transfer jig*. This consists of three channelled clamping devices for holding dopsticks: two in line with each other and separated by a gap and the third (which may be omitted, see Fig 33) facing towards the middle

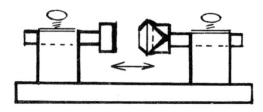

FIG 33 Transfer jig

of the gap at right angles to the line of the other two. It mounts a flat-headed dopstick and serves for truing the dopped stone.

The procedure is to clamp a newly dopped stick in either of the two aligned holders while the dopping is still plastic in such a way that the girdle of the preform touches the head of the truing stick. If the stone is well centred it should remain in light touch with the truing stick when rotated.

This description already goes some way to show why it is preferable to work the pavillion first, but an additional reason is that the pavillion, being pointed or convergent, is easier to centre when transferred to a hollow-headed dopstick.

The latter is a delicate operation, because the stone has to be released from one dopstick without shifting its position and accurately mounted on another. The two sticks are aligned in the transfer clamps, the receiving one carrying a head of dopping wax in plastic condition. The stone must be sufficiently warm—and preferably coated with shellac—to adhere to this dopping wax, without, how-

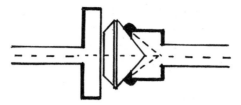

FIG 34 Face-plate (in transfer jig) used for checking alignment of the crown in a pavillion-dopped brilliant

ever, losing its seat on the old dop. The sticks are slid into contact along the holding channel, and if all goes well the stone will be accurately dopped on both sticks. The wax must be allowed to harden. This done, the stone has to be released from the old dop, which, being of metal and a good heat conductor, can be exposed to a spirit or bunsen flame at some distance from the stone, so as slowly to raise its temperature until the wax at contact with the stone becomes plastic. In the cold dopping method a solvent is applied instead.

The stone may then be checked up for alignment in the way already described.

CUTTING THE FACETS

The remark that facetting is difficult is trite, but true. Just look at those minute triangles, trapezia, pentagons and what have you, all of them perfectly matched in size, angle and placement. Intimidating, isn't it? The reader, however, may draw some encouragement from the following observation by Glenn and Martha Vargas in their book *Faceting for Amateurs* (p 200): 'The professional must turn his time into money, and perfection is secondary. The amateur is willing to put much time into the achieving of a perfect gem.' 'Amateur' is derived from the Latin *amator*, meaning 'lover'—the lover of the work he does.

Perfection is a matter of patient and painstaking trying; and clearly it would be inadvisable to use good expensive material or to embark on a complicated cutting pattern in the first attempt. A fairly large stone will be easier to work than a small one. The table cut is the simplest of all possible patterns and may be followed by the commercial cut (p 64) or the spinning wheel (p 63) among the 'round' gems, although the standard instructions are given here for the round octagonal brilliant.

The stone is so placed upon the lap that the quill slopes in the direction of rotation. The facetting head is slewably mounted upon the mast, so that the stone can sweep the lap with arcuate motion. This is important for conserving the lap, the uniform use of the abrasive, and the uniform cutting action on the facet, for it will be recalled that the cutting speed increases towards the edge of the lap, so that, other things being equal, the part of the stone facing away from the centre will be cut deeper, giving the facet an unwanted slope. Step cuts are particularly sensitive to this fault, as the sides of each step must be exactly parallel to each other. On the other hand, the outer parts of the lap tend to be used more than the central, which in an old lap will have more and sharper abrasive and so greater cutting power. All this has to be borne in mind.

The dopstick is held in hand close to the stone, and, consequently, the pressure applied to it is manually controlled. In a horizontal facetting machine it will thus be greater at high inclinations than at low ones, and lowest for the girdle facets, when the quill lies parallel to the lap surface. This, too, must be taken into account.

Too little pressure produces *undercutting*, which is not a serious fault, as it is corrected simply by further cutting. Too much pressure, apart from the danger of overheating and preventing the lubricant entering under the stone, may lead to *overcutting*, which makes the facet relatively too large and out of joint with its neighbours. The overcutting can be corrected only by similarly overcutting all the other facets, thus reducing the size of the finished gem; or else the facet angles may have to be altered, which is permissible within narrow limits, but generally inadvisable.

The grade of the lap will vary with the size of the facet. Only large facets on large stones are started on a coarse lap. It need not be used

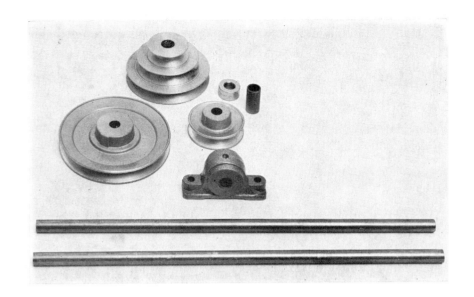

Page 131 (*above*) Machine parts: pulleys, plummer block (½in bore with graphite impregnated bore), bush for same and collar with grub screw; (*below*) cutting a facet on a round brilliant preform

Page 132 (*above*) PMR 4 (British) combination unit, with saw blade and grinding wheel in position; (*below*) Star Diamond Model GP-6 (American) combination unit

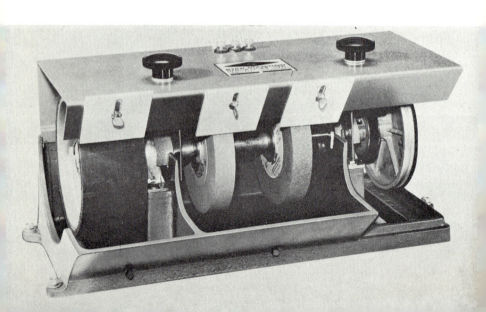

at all for smaller facets and stones not exceeding a few carats in weight. A coarse lap may be employed for the table, but a medium followed by a fine one will do for all the other facets, and the smallest facets, such as the corner facets of the emerald and similar cuts, require the fine lap alone.

Abrasive hygiene must be stringently observed. The indexing and inclination settings must be impeccable. As the cutting progresses, constant inspection of the stone is necessary, especially towards the end of the operation, when pressure and cutting action have to be reduced, to keep clear of the dangerous mark where the facet is overcut. Wherever we have a row of equal facets it is advisable to cut alternate facets first, and then interpose the intermediate ones. This reduces the risk of misalignment. It will also help not to cut the facets to full depth at the first go, but to undercut the whole row, leaving narrow bridges or uncut corners between the adjoining facets, which can be closed on a finer lap at the second go.

Some lapidarists do start with the crown, but reasons have already been given for preferring the opposite cutting order. An additional consideration is that the culet facets must have the correct inclination, to avoid the 'fish-eye' effect (p 37), and with the pavillion properly completed this hurdle has been safely taken. The mains or the large culet steps are cut first, and then the breaks, or such other facets as there may be, to reach the girdle.

A knife-edge at the girdle must be avoided, as it is easily chipped and is awkward to set in jewellery. If the preform is ground to a cylinder the girdle may be left unpolished, but there are various considerations in favour of having it facetted. For one thing this gives the gem a neater, more finished appearance. For another if the girdle facets are accurately aligned with the pavillion break facets it is easier to bring the crown breaks into coincidence with them.

In a spinning wheel cut, all facets are isosceles triangles meeting at the culet and crown points respectively (no table). The number of the facets may vary, but the angle remains the same in each half of the gem, and only the indexing needs attention.

In the commercial cut there are no star facets, and the pavillion

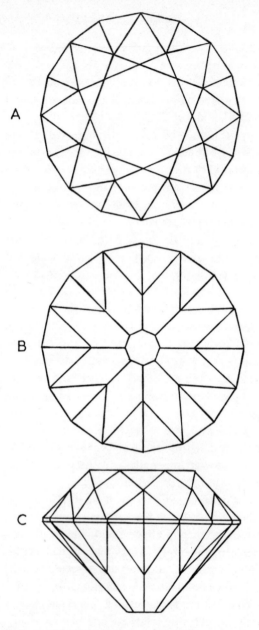

FIG 35 Standard round brilliant with culet table: A = crown; B = pavillion; C = side view

and crown mains meet at the girdle. In fact, the two halves are identical, save for the crown being cut to half-height by the table. This makes an ideal configuration for a beginner.

Tradition will have it, however, that we start with the octagonal standard brilliant, so here it is. We may assume that we have a conical preform of quartz, which is easy to work (no cleavage, excessive heat sensitivity, and so on) and comparatively inexpensive, so that obtaining a crystal of good size does not present a serious problem. We use an index of eightfold symmetry and an angle setting of $43°$ for the pavillion mains. The beginners are recommended to start off by cutting four alternate, instead of the required eight, pavillion mains, making a cross at the culet on a coarse lap. The main object of the exercise is to get the culet point accurately centred. With this accomplished, the four intervening mains are cut so as to meet at the culet. Since this is the first stage of processing, it is better slightly to undercut the facets, to allow for the removal of material in the fine-working and polishing operations. Should, however, any of the facets come out overcut, the remaining ones must be cut to the same depth to restore the balance. There will be roughly triangular uncut areas near the girdle, extending down along the edges of the facets, but so long as they do not go beyond about a quarter of the length of the latter this does not matter, as all such roughnesses will be eliminated when the breaks are cut.

These are $2-6°$ steeper than the mains, indexed $\frac{1}{16}$ of the revolution of the indexer ahead, and may be done consecutively or alternately. In the finished state they usually reach halfway to the culet, but when first cut on a medium or fine lap they will be somewhat longer, to allow for the subsequent paring. The result should be an eight-pointed star when viewed from the culet. The mains are now reworked on the fine lap, to remove the coarse scratches and correct minor errors, if any.

The outline of the girdle will probably be an imperfect circle, and the points of the mains should preferably fall somewhat short of it, and in no case beyond it. At this stage it will be of advantage to cut the girdle facets on the same index setting and $0°$ inclination, so that they terminate exactly at the points of the mains, and leave them unpolished. The whole of the pavillion can now be redone on the fine lap, where necessary, and polished.

The gem is thus ready for reversing in the way described on pp 128 ff and for working the crown. Once the stone has been redopped, advantage may be taken of the girdle facets, to ensure accurate indexing. The dopstick is left loose in the quill, or if this is not possible in some makes —the quill is uncoupled from the indexer, the inclination set at o°, and a girdle facet allowed to come to rest freely upon a motionless polishing lap. This should ensure the correct indexing for the break facets, which can be tested by moving the stone gently over the lap. The movement will impart a touch of polish to the facet. If it lies truly flat upon the lap the shine will be uniformly distributed; if not and the shine appears at one edge only the attitude of the dop needs adjusting. The index position is then secured.

This, though, corresponds to the break facets and not to the mains that come next, and so the indexer will have to be turned once more through $\frac{1}{16}$ of a revolution. The angle of the crown mains is 42°, and they are cut on the medium lap, with a slight undercutting as before, and when checked up and found in order recut on the fine lap.

Now it is the turn of the table, which requires an angular setting of 90°, best obtained by means of the 45° dop (p 112). The work is started off on the coarse lap and taken right through to final polish. In the finished gem the table will extend to 50 per cent of the width, but again an allowance must be made for the removal of material at the edges when the star facets are cut on the fine lap at the next stage. The table is, therefore, given a 10 per cent extra width, which should be accurately measured. The index setting for the star facets is the same as for the break and girdle facets, and the angle is 27°.

The break facets are cut last on the fine lap; their angle is about 18° more than the 42° of the crown mains. It is not fixed, and must be determined by trial and error so that the apices of the break triangles touch those of the star facets, and their bases coincide with the corners of the crown mains, on the one hand, and of the pavillion breaks, on the other. Care must also be taken not to eat up too much of the girdle, which should be of a uniform breadth all round the gem.

When this operation has been successfully carried out, all the crown facets are checked up, corrected if necessary, and given the final polish. It must be emphasised, however, that polishing is unsuited to correcting anything but very minor faults, so that any mistakes must be put right on the fine lap.

These instructions can be readily adapted to the commercial cut, which is a simplified version of the standard brilliant, and the procedure in making a step cut is closely comparable.

One problem that may be encountered at the polishing stage is that of *aggregation and flow*. The abrasive and stone dust tend to collect in a mound on the lap at the head of movement of the stone. This may give the facet a rounded edge. Moreover, as the lap revolves fast, a partial vacuum is created under the stone into which the mound of abrasive is sucked up, cutting out a groove in the facet. Adequate lubrication, moving the stone about the lap and reducing the cutting speed and pressure, should conquer these difficulties, which do not arise on a permanently charged diamond lap, nor on a vertical disc.

9

MORE ABOUT MACHINES

A COMBINATION UNIT IS A MACHINE ASSEMBLY EMBODYING PARALLEL or exchangeable appliances for performing more than one lapidary task. There is a wide range of such machines on the market, and it is not possible to give here more than a representative cross section of the various makes and designs. This is as unbiased as is humanly possible, but a selection of this kind is to some extent governed by accessibility and chance; and while reasonable care has been taken to include only reliable machinery worthy of recommendation, an author is not in a position to test every advertised article and must accept some of the manufacturers' statements on trust. Many excellent machines are excluded from the review simply for reasons of space.

Ultimately the reader must reply on his own judgment. A flashy advertisement is no guarantee of good performance, nor is price as such, although technical refinements cost money and must inevitably be reflected in it. Cutting stones is hard work, and to do it reliably for a long time, requires a sturdy construction. Accurate machining of parts is another important point. Both of these can be judged from photographs, bearing in mind the correct scale, with reference to description.

The simplest combination unit consists of a trimming saw and a grinding wheel mounted at the opposite ends of the same shaft and usually driven through belt and pulley located between them. The grinding wheel is made exchangeable for a wheel of different grade, a sanding disc or a polishing buff as and when required.

A good example of such a unit is the British-made PMR 4 (see plate, p 132). The frame is made of solid aluminium castings through-out and measures 13 × 11in across and is 10½in high. The outfit comprises a 6 × 0·32in diamond saw blade; two interchangeable 6 × 1in grinding wheels of grades 80 and 220; plywood sanding discs of grades 320 and 400 with spare sheets; a 6in leather and a 6in hard-felt buff; cerium oxide, dopsticks, dopping wax and an aluminium pencil. The design includes a 3-jaw chuck, grit-proof ball-races, splash shields and saw guards. A ⅓HP motor is recommended by the manufacturers. The machine is reasonably priced. The *American Rock Rascal Model T* is a similar unit, and there are others that are largely equivalent.

The *Star Diamond Model GP-6* (American, marketed in Britain by Wessex Impex Ltd), shown on p 132, is a larger more complicated grinder-polisher. The assembly includes a drum sander and two 6 × 1in grinding wheels with adjustable splash-guards, as well as three control valves for regulating the flow of coolant. In addition, this machine has a wheel mounted at the end of the extended shaft, for the reception of sanding and polishing discs, but no trim saw, which, however, is incorporated in the British PMR 3 and 5 (see plate, p 149) that are otherwise similar except for the absence of a drum sander and the presence of a tank for the coolant, arranged over the grinding wheels. Various accessory items are covered by the purchase price.

The photograph on p 149 illustrates another embodiment of the same general idea by Highland Park Manufacturing Company (American, distributed in Great Britain by Ammonite Ltd, of Cowbridge, Glamorgan, Wales). It is larger—base measurements 12 × 33in, shipping weight 125lb—sturdier and much more expensive.

The *Model E10* comprises a 9 × 0·40in diamond saw, mounted in a tray with a feed clamp and a lateral cross-feed plate for accurate slicing; two 8 × 1½in silicon-carbide grinding wheels of grade 100 and 220 respectively under a duraluminium hood with coolant valves and ducts; an 8in sanding disc, replaceable by an 8in leather buff, at the right end of the assembly; and an 8 × 3in drum sander, which can be fitted in the place of the latter by removing the sanding guard. The drains and splash pan for the saw are located at the back of the machine, which is driven by a $\frac{1}{2}$HP motor (not included) through a V-belt and pulley gear between the saw and the grinders. A special feature is the wheel dresser support, slidable on a shaft in front of the grinding wheels. Self-aligning pillow-block ball bearings ensure smooth and quiet running.

Larger units, such as this, with permanently mounted wheels and saws, save a lot of trouble, but also cost more and occupy more room. In the final analysis our choice will depend on the available funds and space, and on how much material we intend to handle. An amateur with only a few stones to cut and polish can afford to fiddle about exchanging discs, and logically the process of simplification leads to a compact, versatile unit where everything from saw blade to polishing buff is exchangeably mounted on a single snub axle. Naturally, something of what is gained on the swings is lost on the roundabouts: such machines require certain ancillary gadgets, as well as greater care and working skill.

This has been the engineering guide-line in the design of 'mini units' put on the market by M. L. Beach, of Twickenham, Middlesex, England. We will consider here two of his machines, intended to tackle any lapidary job, from slicing and trimming to facetting and polishing: the 'improved' *Gem Master* and the *Facet Master*, which represent a horizontal and a vertical solution of the problem respectively.

The *Gem Master* weighs approximately 10lb bare (without accessories), and measures $12\frac{1}{2} \times 11$in in horizontal and 12in in vertical extension. The frame of cast aluminium is a deep rectangular tray standing on four legs, which can be screwed on to a bench or table. Mounted within the tray is a $\frac{5}{8}$in vertical steel arbor, supporting a horizontal spun-aluminium turntable of 6in diameter, which will accept a lap or grinding wheel up to 7in across. A 3in pulley driving the turntable is located underneath the tray and connected by a V-belt transmission to $\frac{1}{6}$–$\frac{1}{3}$HP electric motor. There is a mini version of this machine intended for 4in discs.

To use the machine as a trimming saw, the turntable is removed and replaced by a 2½in adapter, which is screwed on to the shaft and supports the blade, held in position from above by a large washer and a finger nut. It is very important in any mounting for the blade to run true without lateral wobble, and this is doubly so in the case of a horizontal blade. It must, therefore, be turned into various positions, to see that it stays parallel to the bottom of the tray. The stone is held in a 'stone slicing clamp', which does not differ substantially from the usual type of feed vice, but is slewably mounted upon a vertical mast, set in a threaded opening provided for this purpose in the base of the tray. The vertical position of the clamp can be adjusted by means of a movable collar which supports it from below.

Such blade mounting is less handy than the usual vertical type, but it does not present any insuperable difficulty. The machine will take a 6in blade. A large polythene can with a lid, tap and feed pipe is provided beside the tray for coolant (water) or lubricant.

One hundred and 220 silicon-carbide grinding discs, charged diamond laps, and a hard-felt polishing lap with cerium oxide are interchangeably used. The facetting device operates on the O'Brien principle (p 114). It consists of a vertical rod or mast, similar to that used for the 'slicing clamp' and mounted in the same way, a facetting table, which can be secured at various heights upon the mast and supports an O'Brien template, fixed by a wing nut to the rear of the dopstick. Three templates are provided: a square, a pentagonal and a hexagonal one. The side of the template rests free upon the table, and the angle of the facet is determined by the height of the table and the length of the dopstick. The facet angle is equal to the angle the template substends with the table, and must be measured with a separate protractor. So far so good, but as the facet is ground down the effective length of the dopstick will change, making the angle steeper. If no adjustment is made, not only will the angle be wrong, but the facet will tend to acquire a cylindrical surface through uneven cutting. These tendencies have to be carefully watched and corrected. A further difficulty arises from the fact that the lap cuts faster towards the periphery. The manufacturer recommends pressing the far end of the dopped stone down with a finger, to make up for the difference in cutting speed. I have no doubt that satisfactory results can be obtained in this way, but this requires some skill and practice, which are unnecessary with a conventional facetting head where the inclination of the dopstick is rigidly fixed. Against this must be set that the whole unit costs less than such a head alone.

For cutting an octagonal gem a square template is used to cut alternate facets and then turned through $45°$ for the intermediate foursome. The pentagonal and hexagonal templates can be similarly manipulated for ten- and twelve-sided cuts. There exists no fundamental obstacle to mounting an indexing head upon the *Gem Master's* mast.

The *Facet Master* is a real mini. Its overall dimensions are: $6 \times 6\frac{1}{2}$in horizontal and $5\frac{1}{2}$in vertical; weight 4lb. The mounting is vertical, and all wheels, including the saw, are of 4in diameter. The facetting arrangement is of especial interest (see plate, p 150): it is a combination of the O'Brien idea and an indexing head. The dopstick itself is fat and of polygonal cross-section: square, hexagonal, etc. There is also a cylindrical dop with twenty-four equispaced longitudinal grooves, which allow corresponding indexing by means of a 'finger', secured by a screw to a side of a box-like clamp that holds the dopstick. The clamp has three bores fitting a vertical mast, slidable in a slot alongside the cutting wheel. Once more the angle of the facet has to be measured with a protractor and is determined by the effective length of the dopstick from the wheel face to the centre of the clamp. This distance can be varied by moving the dopstick inside the clamp and passing the mast through any of the three bores. As stated, the mast itself is slidable along the cutting face, and the clamp is free to move up and down along it, so that the position of the facet on the face of the wheel can be varied without affecting the facet angle. This eliminates some of the objections to the earlier arrangement, but the angle must be frequently checked as before.

The listed accessories include: 100 and 280 silicon-carbide grinding wheels, which are worked mainly on the flat side like laps;

hard felt wheel; perspex wheel; cast-iron 'lap wheel'; copper 'lap-wheels' charged with diamond abrasive—coarse on one side only, medium and fine on alternate sides; and a 'special lapidary diamond saw blade'. The water supply is in a tank underneath the wheel as in conventional saws, but, except for sawing, such lubrication is excessive, and it is suggested placing in the tank strips of sponge plastic 4 × 1¼ × ½in imbued with water, in contact with the operative side of the wheel. This method is effective with diamond wheels, but silicon-carbide wheels have to be moistened from a 'squeezy bottle'; too much water may cause them to disintegrate under the centrifugal force of rotation, which can be dangerous—a rule of general validity, regardless of machine design.

The London firm Whithear Lapidary Company has produced a larger version of a 'universal machine', Model WL1, which can handle anything from sawing to facetting. The latter is likewise done on a vertical disc by means of a graduated indexing head of a more conventional design.

A mini unit of this kind is certainly more difficult to operate effectively than a large compound machine, but it is economical and may repay the trouble of learning its idiosyncrasies. It should not be beyond the skill of an amateur constructor to build a compound unit of his own on similar lines.

A HOME-MADE MACHINE

An amateur lapidary's workshop with a home-made combination unit is illustrated on p 150. The amateur, Ken Attwood, of Aviemore, Scotland, is a mechanical engineer in real life, but this need not discourage the reader from following his example.

The assembly comprises four operative elements mounted on the same mainshaft, which is driven by a ¼HP motor obtained from an old refrigerator. The motor is protected by a thermal overload trip switch and slung underneath the machine frame on a vertically and horizontally adjustable mounting, to accommodate changes in the length of the V-belt when different transmission ratios are used. For this purpose there are three grooves on the motor pulley and four on the mainshaft pulley, giving eight different speeds. The lowest speed of 470rpm is used for polishing.

The operative elements are from left to right: an $8 \times 1\frac{1}{2}$in felt buff, a $7 \times 1\frac{1}{2}$in grinding wheel, an $8 \times 1\frac{1}{2}$in grinding wheel, and a sanding drum. The two outside elements are housed separately and each is secured to the mainshaft by two grub screws, so that they can be readily removed. In addition, their housings are detachably clamped to the machine frame, and the front part of the buff housing is removable as well, to allow the buff to be replaced by a polishing disc. The buff is normally slipped off when not in use. The grinding wheels are housed in the middle compartment, which is in two parts, to facilitate exchange.

Water is delivered to the wheels from an overhead tank through needle valves, and the waste drains off into a container on the floor through a $\frac{1}{2}$in plastic tube.

The 1in steel shaft has been turned down to $\frac{7}{8}$in between the two grinding wheels and threaded to accept the nuts securing the wheels and drums. It has been further reduced to $\frac{3}{4}$in in unthreaded portions, and runs in two self-aligning ball races on the two sides of the central compartment housing the grinding wheels. The parts of the shaft passing through the inside walls of the outer compartments have a diameter of $\frac{1}{2}$in. The pullies are protected by a forwardly hinged perspex guard.

The housings are made of a gauge six aluminium alloy sheet, which was folded, using hardwood blocks, G clamps and a wooden mallet. All joints were drilled and riveted by hand, and corners filled with plastic metal. The edges of the splash pans were seamed and wired by hand. The machine base is made with $2 \times 1 \times \frac{1}{2}$in rectangular tubes, and the stand with $2\frac{1}{4}$in pinewood slats.

Shafts, pulleys, ball races, etc can be purchased from lapidary outfitters, as can wheels, laps, drums and other exchangeable parts. The latter were indeed bought, and the total outlay on the machine was about £16 ($38). The work required the use of a lathe for the shaft and some minor items, a threading tap, a drill, and such common tools as screwdrivers, pliers, etc. It is estimated to have involved between 160 and 170 man-hours.

This machine has performed very satisfactorily during several years of constant use. Ken Attwood observes that the standard K-bond grinding wheels are too hard for working with quartz and materials of similar hardness, unless run at speeds below 1,600rpm. They tend to glaze and run out of true. Soft-bonded wheels are preferable and cut faster, but there is a danger of the stone becoming embedded in the wheel and being carried along by it, which could cause injury to the operator and damage to the machine. The stone must be applied to the soft wheel with very little pressure.

A combination unit built by a metal-working class is described in great detail, with diagrams and photographs, in John Wainwright's book, *Discovering Lapidary Work*.

SPECIALISED MACHINERY

So far in this chapter the accent has been on universality, but a specialised machine, constructed for doing one particular job to the maximum attainable perfection, has a legitimate place in a lapidary workshop, more particularly in larger establishments, clubs, schools, etc where more than one person is at work at the same time, although an individual enthusiast, too, may wish to concentrate on some special aspect of lapidary work, say facetting, tumbling or cutting cabochons.

Facetting and tumbling machines are such specialised appliances and are dealt with in more detail in the corresponding chapters. It will, however, be seen that a cabochon can be cut on a facetting lap by the simple trick of not using a facetting head, and a facetting head, perhaps with some modifications, can be fitted to a general-purpose machine. On the other hand, a slabbing saw could not be adapted to do any work other than that implied in its name, except possibly trimming.

The *VL* 10 vibrating lap by Star Diamond Industries Inc (American, marketed in Britain by Wessex Impex) is a further example of a specialised lapidary appliance (see plate, p 167). Frame apart, it consists of an aluminium cast grid pan, 10in in diameter, mounted in suspension on helical springs, with a rubber bumper ring insert. The lap is charged with loose abrasive mixed with water, and set in a circular oscillation of small amplitude by an inbuilt fan-cooled motor. The stones are laid loose upon the surface of the lap and are cut to a flat finish. The lap is not suitable for accurate facetting, but is effective for fashioning large flat surfaces, such as agate slabs. For polishing the lap is replaced by a woven fabric impregnated with paste made with a polishing agent.

VI-BRO-LAP from Ammonite Ltd, Cowbridge, Glamorgan, is a larger and heavier machine constructed on a similar principle. The makers claim that it 'eliminates the necessity for many runs of progressively smaller grits . . . The patented suspension and grooving allows the grits to get under the work where they are crushed to progressively smaller sizes, cutting all the time.' This machine belongs to the more expensive type of equipment.

Cutting cabochons is one of the easiest and most popular lapidary pursuits, and various machines have been designed with it in view. On p 94 mention has been made of diamond-charged, convexly surfaced, wooden drums for cabochon work. Several machines based on this principle are commercially available, and may be exemplified by the Model 6XL (see plate, p 167), manufactured by Dorothy Blake Custom Jewelry, of Los Angeles, California.

The overall dimensions of the machine, including that $\frac{1}{40}$HP motor which works on a 115V, 60 cycle alternating current at a single speed of 1,500rpm, are 9 × 19 × 4½in. The shipping weight is 12lb. The price with the motor is comparable to that of a medium-sized combination unit. The design is very simple. Six drums, or spools, of laminated maple wood are seated on a common shaft, and are driven jointly by V-belt and single pulley transmission. The perimeters of the drums have a flat section occupying about a third of their width, the remaining part being convexly profiled with variable curvature.

The processing order is from left to right, and the last three drums are equipped with a special narrow groove for working the edge of the cabochon. On the left side of the frame in line with the motor there is a shelf with six apertures for the reception of six syringes and a holder for a bottle of charging (extender) fluid. The syringes hold a diamond abrasive paste, marketed under the name of 'Crystalite Diamond Compound', one gramme each of the four coarser grades: 325, 600, 1,200 and 8,000, and two grammes of the polishing grades: 14,000 and 50,000 (see p 71). These are recommended and supplied by the makers, but other preparations may be used, for instance, the British MK Diamond Compounds: 325 brown, 600 tan, 1,000 purple, 8,000 orange, 14,000 pink, and 28,000 ivory.

The method of charging the drums consists in applying one at a time a small dab of paste from the appropriate syringe, about $\frac{1}{16}$in as it comes out of the nozzle, to a stone in the process of cutting, and working it into the wood, so as to evenly cover the entire operative perimeter. According to the manufacturer's instructions, the first stone will need, depending on its size, three to six dabs for even distribution. A drop of extender will help to spread the abrasive. The stone must be carefully cleaned for the next drum, where the same operation is repeated with a syringe of a successively finer grade. The manufacturer recommends using 'toilet tissue' for cleaning the stone, but there can be no harm in washing it, so long as it is properly dried afterwards. The same tissue should never be used for cleaning different grades, and abrasive hygiene is especially important with a machine of this type.

Once a few stones have been worked, the drums should not need recharging for some time. It is a mistake to overcharge them. They should be worked evenly for long life, using the grooves for the sides of the cabochon and finishing the job on the flat section. It must be remembered that diamond abrasive works strictly on the principle of mineralogical scratch, so that the only pressure required is that needed to keep the stone in contact with the drum. If these instructions are scrupulously followed the recommended set of six syringes should last for about five years. This makes diamond abrasives economical in the long run.

In case of accidental contamination of a finer by a coarser grade (the reverse is harmless) the injunction is to wipe the affected part clean with a cloth imbued with the extender fluid and then work on it with a hard stone (eg agate) this time applying pressure, to drive the coarse grit particles deep into the wood. If this does not work the drum has to be replaced, as it cannot be cleaned up on a lathe because the diamond would damage the cutter.

The machine uses little power and makes very little noise, so that it can be used in a living room. The waste is reduced to a minimum; there is no lubricant and so no sludge. Nevertheless, stone flour will accumulate under the drums, and will have to be removed from time to time. The shaft is held by nuts and can be lifted out together with the drums.

The machine is credibly claimed to be very effective for dealing with difficult materials, such as turquoise and opal, and to be free from the orange-peel effect (see p 98). It is designed, however, for sanding and polishing only, and so is not self-sufficient: the sawing, trimming and grinding have to be done separately. Another snag from the point of view of the prospective British buyers is that the motor supplied by the manufacturer cannot be worked off the British mains (230–250V and 50 cycles), and will have to be replaced or adjusted.

The use of diamond-charged wooden drums is not a proprietary feature of the machine. In fact, a very similar machine, the *ADP-18 Super Polisher*, has been produced by the Canadian firm Apex Minerals & Lapidary, of Vancouver, BC, and there are others. Most of the above description and hints will apply to all of them, with such minor modifications as some special features of the design may require and will be found in the manufacturer's instructions supplied with the machine.

The upper photograph on page 168 illustrates a further example of a highly specialised machine. This British machine, produced by the already mentioned London firm Whithear Lapidary Company, serves solely for grinding out part-spherical depressions in flat stone slabs intended for ashtrays. The motor, mounted to be adjustable in

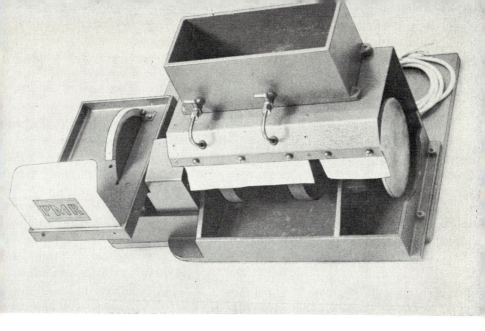

Page 149 (*above*) PMR 5 (British) combination unit, including 6in diamond saw, two 6in × 1in grinding wheels (100 and 220), 1 felt and 1 leather buff, 2 sanding discs (320 and 400) with a spare sheet each, and minor accessories; (*below*) Highland Park (American) Model E-10 combination unit with accessories

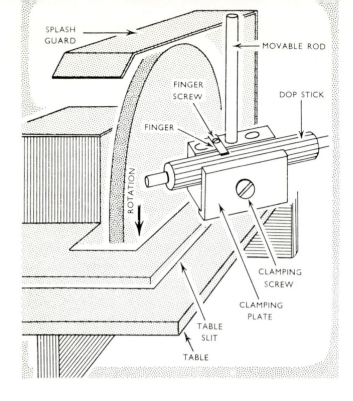

SPLASH GUARD

MOVABLE ROD

FINGER SCREW

DOP STICK

FINGER

ROTATION

CLAMPING SCREW

CLAMPING PLATE

TABLE SLIT

TABLE

Page 150 (above) Facet Master
(British) combination unit;
(right) Ken Attwood's combination unit and workshop

height and inclination at one end of a sloping arm, drives a diamond wheel up to 6in in diameter at the other end of the arm, which is brought to bear against the workpiece clamped to a revolving disc in a hexagonal splash tray. Provisions are made for the supply of coolant and removal of waste.

There are special machines for beads, spheres and 'eggs', as well as machine tools for stone carving and other specialised equipment which exceeds the scope of the present work. Tumbling machinery is considered in the next chapter.

10

TUMBLING

TUMBLING IS THE SIMPLEST FORM OF LAPIDARY WORK. IT CALLS FOR very little skill, or indeed effort, on the part of the operator, as the process is largely automatic, and his intervention is sporadic and almost wholly limited to maintenance and supervision. The technique is an adaptation and controlled development of the natural processes of beach and river erosion which convert jagged screes into smooth, rounded pebbles.

The mechanical ingredients are: a watertight container which is kept in gentle but constant motion, either rotary or vibratory; a mechanism that controls this motion; and, of course, a source of power, ie an electric motor with appropriate gearing (see plate, p 168). The 'erosion' takes place in the container, which holds the stones, water and abrasive, with such other ingredients as may expedite or temper its operation.

On the beach or river bed the natural abrasive is sand. In a tumbling drum or barrel it is almost exclusively silicon carbide. Nobody would dream of tumbling diamonds or rubies, nor for that matter beryls, unless these be of a very poor grade, so that the hardness of the tumbling material seldom exceeds grade seven. In fact, this material is chiefly chalcedonic silica. Minerals with strongly developed cleavage are obviously unsuitable for tumbling, as they will tend to disintegrate in the process. Also those with a brightly coloured streak, eg haematite, although not impossible to tumble, are very messy to handle, and therefore, not to be recommended. The object of the exercise is to produce pretty pebbles, so that the tumbling charge must be 'pebblesome'. It usually consists of opaque or translucent material, but sub-standard, flawed crystals which are unsuitable for cutting are also eligible.

The stones in the charge must be of the same hardness, or else the softer ones would be worn away before the harder are ground smooth, and of approximately the same size, although it is useful to include some pea-sized ones, which act like ball bearings between the larger pebbles and expedite contact between them and the abrasive grit. It is better not to mix hammer-broken matter with water-worn material, where the job has already been half-done by nature.

Tumbling action largely depends on gravity, and becomes in-effective if there is not enough weight. If we are short of suitable stones appropriate ballast must be provided. It should match the hardness of the main charge as nearly as possible. Flint or quartz balls will do for silica, but not for serpentine. On the other hand, the stones must tumble over and over, and so need room to move. A rotary drum is charged between half and two-thirds full for effective tumbling. In a vibratory drum this is less important, and it can accept more material, although it too would fail if jammed full. The process is slow and takes many days, becoming progressively slower as the size of the tumbler decreases. While it would be possible to operate a mini-tumbler 2 or 3in across, this would take much too long, and the diameter of 6in sets a practical lower limit to a tumbling drum.

If the process were allowed to continue for long enough the stones would emerge more or less perfectly round. But there are limits to human patience and an acceptable bill for electricity, so that usually the first tumbling phase is deemed complete as soon as the stones have lost their rough edges, sharp corners and surface snags. This results in an artistic variety of shape, which is often more pleasing to the eye than dull uniformity, though it, too, has its limitations.

Tumbling, like any other lapidary operation, aims at imparting to the stones a progressively smoother surface, until they are ready to accept final polish. Consequently, the same precepts, including those of abrasive hygiene, continue to apply. There are normally two stages corresponding to grinding and one to sanding, for which a succession of grits of grades 80, 120 and 400, or 120, 320 and 500, is commonly employed. It will be understood that the grain size may be varied within narrow limits, so long as the progression is maintained. A pinch of detergent is beneficial.

In passing from a lower to a higher stage the stones have to be carefully inspected and washed. The same applies to the tumbling barrel, and, if possible, it is preferable to have separate barrels for every grade of abrasive. The use of rubber gloves is advisable for reasons of abrasive hygiene and for protection when working with brittle materials, such as obsidian which tends to splinter into needle-sharp sherds.

The tumbling process is accompanied by considerable evolution of gas. This does not present a serious problem if commercial poly-thene drums and 'rubber liners' are used, but hermetically sealed metal or wooden barrels may blow up, like bottles with fermenting fruit juice, unless the gas pressure is periodically relieved, which is known as 'burping'. A 6in drum of such construction has to be 'burped' once every 24 hours; larger containers require less frequent attention.

A daily inspection of the tumbler is necessary in any case for other reasons. There should be just enough water to cover up the charge of stones and abrasive, the latter being about 10 per cent of the weight of the stones (for silica, less for softer materials). But water evaporates and may need replenishing. Abrasive, too, gets used up as the tumbling goes on, and more important, stone waste accumulates and forms a sticky slurry which effectively immobilises the stones and so prevents grinding action. This cannot be allowed to happen, and should such a situation begin to threaten the stones must be removed, washed and recharged with new water and abrasive. Furthermore, not all stones in the charge will reach completion simultaneously; some will be ready for transfer into the next stage, while others have to stay behind for further treatment. The charge, however, cannot be allowed to drop below the permissible half of the drum's volume, and the deficiency must be made good with new stones or ballast. All this requires intermittent attention.

There is one important point not to be forgotten: tumbling waste makes an excellent cement and will set stone-hard in a couple of hours. For this reason a working tumbler should never be stopped and left standing for more than a few minutes. Similarly pouring away the waste down a sink or a drain may be fraught with dire consequences.

Polishing is the last processing stage. As in previous cases, the stones must be carefully examined and found free from coarse scratches. If not, they should be returned to the third stage for another day's run. If passed, they are scrupulously cleaned of all traces of abrasive and waste, and carefully placed (not just poured in) in the polishing drum with water, a polishing agent and vermiculite or the like, to cushion the load. Some lapidarists recommend adding a cupful of detergent per 5lb of stone, or else syrup or sugar for softer action, but we cannot endorse this.

The proportion of polishing agent is about 1oz to 1lb of stone. Levigated alumina, cerium oxide and tin oxide are commonly used, the last-named being often preferred.

Well-polished stones should be equally shiny, wet or dry. The polishing stage may be usefully followed by a few hours run in a thick mixture of water and detergent, which serves to improve the effect and eliminate all traces of polishing powder. Thereafter the stones are washed in warm running water and dried, and are ready for mounting in jewellery.

MACHINERY

Tumbling machines are simple devices and therefore tempting to an amateur constructor.

The first essential part is a drum, for which any odd tin such as a large paint tin may do, if equipped with a water-tight sealing disc and a lid secured with bolts to prevent its coming off in the working. A wide-necked plastic bottle (the stones inside it should be readily accessible to inspection, etc) with a screwed-on lid is even better. The drum is placed over and between two shafts, which are properly journalled and mounted upon a suitable frame. They lie parallel to each other and about two-thirds of the drum's diameter apart, which ensures stable engagement. One shaft is driven by an electric motor (¼HP or so) over a belt-and-pulley transmission, and the other is freely rotatable but unpowered. As the motor rotates the driven shaft, this entrains the drum which in turn sets the other shaft in rotation. For better engagement and noise abatement the portions of the shaft outside the bearings under the drum may be passed through short lengths of garden hose, or other rubber or plastic tubing, and the drum itself similarly lined by stretching over it three rubber rings cut from an inner tyre tube.

Tin (galvanised iron) is not a good material for a tumbler, unless internally lined with rubber or plastic, as it is very noisy and leaves metallic marks on the stones. Aluminium is even worse, and stains left by it are very difficult to remove—in fact, they have to be polished off. Plastic is good, if sufficiently strong to withstand the wear. So, too, is wood, but it absorbs grit, so that a separate drum is needed for each grade of abrasive. Wooden drums lend themselves to polygonal cross section, which ensures better mixing and so more expeditious tumbling, but is noisier than the conventional circle. Rubber is an ideal material in every respect.

Most home-made drums require burping, and it is questionable whether they are worth the trouble of making, for factory-made rubber, rubber-lined or polythene drums, which are free from this defect, and almost noiseless, as well as durable, are available at moderate prices.

An interesting variant of a home-made tumbling machine, however, has been suggested by Lyn and Ray Cooper in *New Zealand Gemstones*. It makes use of old motor tyre *cases* as tumbling containers. The operative structure consists of a ¼HP electric motor with eg a 2in pulley, to drive by V-belt transmission through a 12–14in pulley a steel shaft, ¾in or so in diameter, over which one, two or three tyre cases are loosely suspended. The shaft must, of course, be journalled and mounted on a firm support, such as a strong kitchen table or bench, and extend sufficiently far beyond it to accommodate the tyres. These are kept from slipping about and off the shaft by means of wooden or plastic discs, screwed on to steel collars, which are fixed to the shaft (see Fig 36).

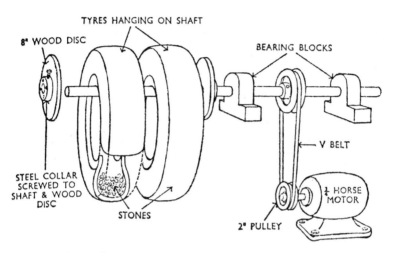

FIG 36 Method of using motor tyres to construct an inexpensive tumbler

The stones, abrasive and water are placed in the bottom hollow part of the tyre case, and tumble over and over as this is entrained in slow rotation.

This arrangement has two signal advantages: it makes comparatively little noise and the container is open to inspection. The concomitant disadvantage is the necessity to keep up the water content, as water evaporates rather rapidly in these conditions. A controlled automatic feed can be provided.

In the case of drum tumblers, too, it is quite a common practice to have more than one container mounted tandem between the shafts.

Vibratory tumblers (see plate, p 185) are more efficient, have a higher loading capacity; the drum is mounted vertically or at a steep angle, and has a lid secured with wing-nuts or the like, so that the operation need not be interrupted for inspection. But they cost about three times as much as the conventional rotary types, and are not equally amenable to do-it-yourself construction.

SPEEDS AND WORKING TIMES

A tumbling barrel, or drum, revolves slowly. The charge is carried some way up the side of the barrel and then rolls back, and this is when the abrasive gets to grips with the stones. If the speed of rotation is too great the stones will be carried swiftly too high up and then drop more or less vertically down. This may cause chipping, and in any case reduces the effectiveness of the grinding action, which depends on their rolling over one another in the same way as when they are swept up and down the seashore by the waves.

Too low a speed causes the stones to slide down too soon, which results in flat-sided, shingle-like shapes. An insufficient load has the same effect. A polygonal drum, however, may stand a considerable reduction in speed. This is not a constant factor in any case, as it depends on the friction between the charge and the inside of the barrel, and so on the nature of the former and the material of the latter. Smooth water-worn pebbles will require higher speeds than angular, hammer-broken material. The same is true if the inside surface of the barrel is smooth.

On rough reckoning the speed works out at 50rpm for an average charge in a 6in round drum (barrel) and 30rpm in an octagonal one; at 10in the corresponding figures drop to some 40 and 25rpm respectively, and so on in inverse ratio to the square root of the radius (or diameter). This applies to rubber-lined or rubber drums. A 25 per cent speed reduction is recommended for the final polishing operation.

In any event a considerable scaling down of the standard motor speed is necessary. Fortunately, rotation is transmitted from the driven shaft to the circumference of the drum, which is thus part of the transmission system. It will be recalled from p 92 that the transmission ratio is equal to that of the diameters (radii) of the input to output pulley, which applies to the present case as well.

Any coating—rubber rings, garden hose, etc—must be included in the count.

Thus if we have a ½in (coated) shaft driving a 10in barrel, the speed reduction will be twentyfold, and this with a motor running at 1,500rpm yields 75rpm, which does not require a large pulley differential to be reduced to the required speed (ie 40rpm).

It will also be observed that the optimal speed and barrel diameter vary inversely to each other, and although the latter appears under a square root, the relationship is approximate only and the root sign may be disregarded for small differences in diameter (say, a transition from 6in to 8in). Thus the speed need not be changed when a somewhat smaller or larger barrel is substituted for the original one. It may be necessary to alter the spacing of the shafts, and since the driven shaft is better left alone, this means adjusting the position of the free one. This can be easily done if it is journalled in bearings movable in a horizontal slot, where they can be fixed at the desired point by means of screws, clamps or other devices.

The processing time at each stage will depend on the nature of the charge and the size of the tumbler. Obviously, the harder the stones the longer they take to be ground smooth. Thus serpentine will be worked twice as fast as agate, but garnet rock will take longer. Sawn or hammer-broken, angular pieces will need more time than water-worn pebbles, and should not be mixed, though pebbles can be used as ballast.

If, however, we take chalcedonic silica (agate, jasper, carnelian, etc) in a 6in round drum, the first two grinding phases will occupy five to six days, and the third (sanding) phase (400–600 grit) about three days. The polishing will again need about five days, but the rinse only one-quarter to one-third of a day.

The noise generated by well-designed tumbling machinery is a good deal less than by normal traffic in our larger towns or cities. Still, it may be disturbing at night, so that it is advisable to keep the machines in a shed or outhouse.

11

DRILLING AND
OTHER REFINEMENTS

THE NEED FOR DRILLING HOLES IN GEMSTONES IS LARGELY LIMITED TO beads and earrings. When the stone is hard it is a difficult job.

The traditional method, which is still is use, employs a *lead-tipped stone drill*, whose thickness varies according to the size of the hole to be made. A thin slit is cut in the lead tip, and two tiny black diamonds, somewhat softer but tougher than the 'white' variety, are carefully fitted close to the opposite ends of the slit under optical magnification. Once their position has been checked up, they are hammered in gently into the lead with a small hammer, and the drill is tried out on glass, to clear the diamonds for action.

The drill is now passed through one of the three holes bored in a thick agate slab, which is mounted on a wooden arm. The dead end of the arm is passed under the operator's left armpit, to control pressure, and the drill is worked horizontally with the right hand by means of an 18in bow-string passed round it. The stones to be drilled are set with dopping wax in rows upon a stone slab. The hole is initiated with a coarser drill (larger diamonds farther apart) and continued with a finer one.

You can try this method if you will, but it is a fair warning that only few candidates can ever master the traditional skill, and much good material is spoiled in the process. As in other cases, however, manual operation may present the advantage of greater control, which is important in dealing with difficult materials, and especially minerals of variable density, such as jasper, agate, turquoise and

160

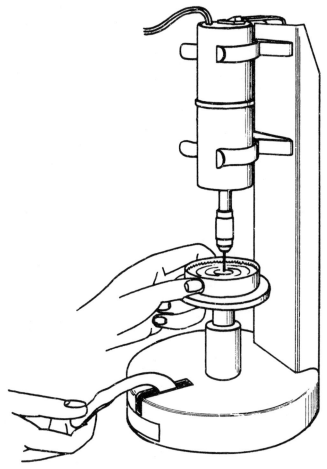

FIG 37 'Beach' drill stand and Titan Drill being used with a diamond
bit, the stone immersed in water, to give cooling and lubrication (M. L. Beach Products Ltd)

lapis lazuli. Cleavage is again a vital consideration, for if a hole were
attempted along a cleavage plane the stone would split.

Softer varieties can be drilled fairly easily with a tungsten-
carbide dentist's burr. A traditional lead-tipped diamond bit can,

of course, be fitted into the chuck of a power-driven drill (see Fig 37). Modern diamond carving points and drill bits can be obtained from lapidary outfitters.

The tube drill is another traditional method of making holes in hard stones. The principle is the same as in sawing stones with a stranded wire and loose abrasive described on p 70. A thin metal tube, which may be of steel or brass, is slightly splayed at the tip and clamped in the chuck of an electric drill. The hole to be drilled is marked on the gem and ringed with a mound of wax or plasticine, or if the gem is small it may be ringed as a whole. The hollow within the mound is filled with a lubricant, which may be light machine oil, turpentine or water, and charged with silicon carbide grit. The grade of the grit depends on the size of the hole: coarse grits of grade 80 or 100 work faster, but not so neatly, and some lapidarists recommend grits as fine as 300. The tube drill is now brought to bear upon the work-piece with a minimum of pressure, and as the tube revolves it picks up the grit and cuts a core in the stone. The drill should be moved up and down, to allow fresh grit to enter under the tube, and frequent inspection is necessary, as stone waste accumulates and fouls the hole, which may have to be cleared.

It is important to have the gem firmly mounted, preferably on a stone block. As in sawing, the delicate stage is reached when the drill is about to break through, as the edges of the hole are likely to be chipped at the exit. To prevent this, the pressure must be reduced, and a stone base is a help, as it obviates the sharp decrease in re-sistance which is the main cause of chipping. Do not mount your gems on wood!

Very fine diamond core bits do exist, but the difficulty of the operation increases with the decreasing diameter of the hole. The drilling machine must be very accurate and the drill run absolutely true and free from vibration, which is a tall order at 4,000rpm— the speed needed to drill agate. It will also be appreciated that the thinner the tube the more likely is it to become blocked by the core, which will be correspondingly the more difficult to remove. Solid diamond bits are less sensitive. Yet even in practised hands a bit has

162

a short useful life, not exceeding twenty $\frac{1}{4}$in deep holes in agate.

On any reckoning fine holes in hard stones are a difficult as well as expensive proposition.

INLAYS, DOUBLETS AND MOSAICS

It is a well-known trick to mount a small diamond within a surround of colourless zircon ('Matura diamond'), to create the impression of a large diamond. The effect is good, and there is nothing wrong about it so long as the article is truthfully described and not passed off for a solid diamond. This is an example of inlay work, the difficulty of which lies in negative cutting.

Making a facetted depression is very difficult, and unnecessary as a hemispherical, conical or cylindrical recess is enough. A cylindrical recess can be accurately cut out with a drill, eg of the core type, all the more easily as its diameter is large as compared with that of a through-hole in a bead, and it is relatively shallow withal. If the inlay is of transparent material the recess must be polished, which can be done, for instance, by mounting in the drill chuck a round hardwood stick of appropriate diameter, charged with diamond powder, or else a felt tongue with cerium oxide or other polishing agent. Special carving and engraving kits are commercially available and may be found useful for such work. Some lubrication will be all the more necessary by reason of the confined working space, and in polishing, the drill must be run at a slow polishing speed (see pp 91 ff).

The next thing is to cut a cylindrical (or other) preform of the inlay material so as to match the recess, polish it, and secure it in the recess with transparent plastic adhesive or Canada balsam, which is used in making compound lenses. If the materials to be matched are not transparent fine polish may be dispensed with. Once the adhesive has set hard, the stone can be cut and polished as one piece.

Strip inlays, crosses or stars can be made in a similar way by using a fine facetting trim saw (p 124). This is one way of making use of odd bits of valuable material.

A simpler job is splicing different stones in a single gem. For example, we may take two pieces of rhodonite and two of azurite, cut two facets at right angles to each other on all of them, so as to make them fit together, and arrange them in alternate sequence. If the facets are accurately cut very little polyester adhesive (eg 'Araldite') will be needed to obtain a firm union between the four pieces, which can then be cut and polished as a single stone, eg in the form of a cabochon or a four-sided pyramid. A Union Jack would make a more ambitious undertaking, but requires no new technique.

There are many other similar possibilities on which to exercise our artistic imagination, but care should be taken that the stones used in the combination are of approximately the same hardness. Simultaneous cutting of a combination of gems widely differing in hardness, though not impossible, is very difficult and not very satisfactory as they would suffer uneven wear later on. This can be done by using very little pressure and/or by shielding the softer components with a hard varnish.

Slices of different materials can be superimposed by the same method and then cut across to give a striped effect, or horizontally for a layered pattern. Doublets are the simplest case in point. Their main application is to opal, especially black opal. A thin slice of opal is cemented to a grey 'potch' rock with a film or plastic adhesive mixed with a black pigment, eg lampblack. Black obsidian may be used instead of potch, as in addition to its colour it matches the hardness of opal—grade six. The cemented doublet is cut into a thin slab or a cabochon with a very low dome.

Other doublets come perilously close to forgery: for instance, when a slice of aquamarine is cemented with a dark-green cement between a crown and pavillion of rock crystal, to imitate an emerald; or else a garnet crown is perched on top of a glass pavillion. However, the dishonesty is neither in the stones nor in the artifacts, but in the use people make of them.

The examples described earlier on may be classed as mosaics, but mosaics proper are structures of greater pictorial complexity, making use chiefly of softer materials, not necessarily gemstones.

164

Amber, coral, mother-of-pearl, malachite, turquoise, but also tortoiseshell and various hardwoods, such as holly, box, lignum vitae, and ebony, are often cemented together with an epoxy adhesive. Emery powder, flour pumice and tripoli are used for polishing the assembled structures.

This is an art in its own right, which, like the engraving and carving of shells and cameos, goes beyond the scope of the present book. Those interested may be referred, for example, to *Carving Shells and Cameos*, by Carson I. A. Ritchie, or other specialised works.

HEAT TREATMENT AND STAINING

Many gemstones change, but mostly lose, their colour upon prolonged exposure to heat. Thus brown-yellow topaz is 'pinked' by being heated in magnesia. The colour at first goes altogether, but a pink shade returns as the stone cools. Yellow topaz, however, shows no comparable recovery and stays colourless. Zircons lose their colour, but gain in sparkle when heated. Most amethysts and cairngorms turn yellow. In fact, many of the commercial citrines have been obtained in this way. Morions, which are a dark peat-brown to black variety of quartz, may usefully be subjected to heat treatment, from which they emerge a rich yellow colour.

There is a Brazilian variety of amethyst which alters from violet to bright green under the influence of heat and is marketed under the name of *vermarine*. The colouring of many agates can be improved by heating, the greys turning to pinks or reds with a general intensification of shadings. The redness of carnelians is enhanced by an application of heat. However, since the brown tints in agates may be due to the same cause as in cairngorms (colloidal silicon) and the violet and purple hues are related to those of amethysts (colloidal iron), they may be destroyed by heating. Rose quartz turns a dull white when heated.

Rapid heating may cause the stones to crack or become clouded through internal fracturing. The application of heat should be very gradual, and it is unwise to exceed 500°F (260°C). The heating is best carried out in a gas or electric oven or furnace, where the temperature can be accurately controlled, with the stones placed in a dish or tin filled with sand. An exposure to maximum temperature of two to three hours should suffice to effect the change of colour.

The colouring of porous minerals, principally agates and other forms of chalcedonic silica, can also be changed by chemical staining. In fact, many of the brightly coloured gems of this kind in the jeweller's window have been so stained. Some of the chemical colourings are permanent, others tend to fade in time; but then the natural colourings of amethyst and topaz are likewise subject to fading on prolonged exposure to sunlight, and the fun is good while it lasts. The temporary hues are usually superficial and imparted to cut stones. In other cases, however, the material is treated raw, and the colour affects the whole mass of the stone, so that it can be cut after treatment like any natural gem.

The simplest case is that of artificial onyx, which can be obtained from any level-banded agate by first keeping it for several days in a hot solution of sugar or syrup, and then soaking in warm sulphuric acid, which burns the absorbed sugar to carbon. Thus, the porous bands turn black while the colour of the compact ones remains unchanged. The stone must, of course, be carefully washed, to remove all traces of the acid. The acquired colouring is permanent.

So, too, is the blue staining produced by steeping in a solution of a ferric salt, followed by immersion in one of yellow or red prussiate of potash (potassium ferrocyanide), which reacts with the ferric salt with the precipitation of Prussian blue (ferric ferrocyanide, $Fe_4[Fe(CN)_6]_3$). The so-called 'Swiss lapis' is produced from red jasper in this way, although other processes which appear to be trade secrets have been used as well with a varying degree of success.

The green colourings are obtained by soaking in a solution either of chromic acid or of a green salt of nickel, such as nickel hydroxide, which is soluble in aqueous ammonia (ie ordinary household ammonia), and subsequent heating. Lemon-yellow hues can be induced by gentle warming in hydrochloric acid in a well-regulated oven for about a fortnight.

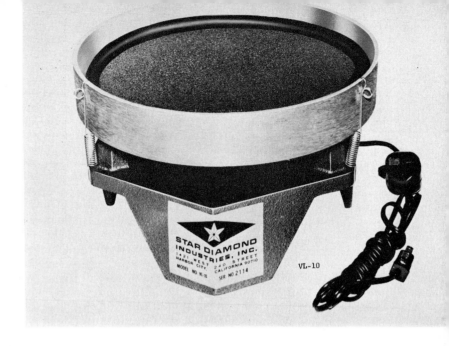

Page 167 (above) Star Diamond VL-10 (American) vibrating lap for dressing flat slabs; (below) Model 6XL (American) cabochon machine by Dorothy Blake Custom Jewelry

Page 168 (left) Ashtray boring machine (British) produced by Whithear Lapidary Company, London, England; (below) Tumbla Master Model F, produced by M L Beach (Products) Ltd. This machine built in two basic units, operating four 1½lb barrels simultaneously, which will conveniently process stones at all stages—three abrasive and final polishing

It should be possible to obtain permanent staining by precipitation of metallic colloids, such as the purple of Cassius, which is colloidal gold of a red to violet colour. It is obtained by adding a very dilute solution of gold chloride to a mixture of stannic and stannous chlorides. In the ensuing reaction hydrated stannic oxide is precipitated and the gold chloride is reduced to pure metal, to which the colour is due.

Turquoise is sometimes chemically stained, to intensify its blue tint, but the effect is not permanent. Another gemstone often subjected to chemical maltreatment is amber, which is stained dark-brown or red by a prolonged application of slow heat and immersion in an appropriate dye.

Crystals do not absorb chemical dyestuffs, and the most one can hope to achieve is a thin surface film, which will not stand up to polishing. Pyrite and some other ores with a metallic lustre can, however, be surface-stained in bright colours by the action of heat in an atmosphere of suitable gas without loss of polish.

12

MAKING JEWELLERY

THE JEWELLER'S ART IS A COMPLICATED SUBJECT THAT REQUIRES A separate book to be dealt with properly, and the present context permits no more than an elementary account of its more accessible aspects. Still, once our stones are cut and polished, it is natural to want to put them to some use, for which it is not necessary to be a Fabergé.

Large stones may make mantelpiece or table ornaments, and be used, for instance, as paperweights. They need be polished on one side only, either as slices (eg agate or malachite) or as more complex, domed, facetted or irregular solids, and ground flat, but left unpolished, at the base to prevent slipping. Thin slices of agate, chalcedony and other translucent minerals, polished on both sides, look attractive when mounted on frosted glass with a strong light behind it, and may have various applications. Obviously a transparent plastic adhesive or Canada balsam should be used to fix the slices to the glass.

Small stones are used mainly as personal ornaments and are intended to be worn either singly or as parts of larger objects, and so require mounting, however simply. The possibilities of cut stones are many and various and will be considered later on. We may usefully attend to the tumble-polished material first, because by its very nature this method involves mass production and creates a corresponding problem of disposal.

Nowadays the situation has been greatly simplified by the so-called *jeweller's* findings (settings), obtainable at reasonable prices from most lapidary suppliers. Findings are mass-produced jewel mountings and parts of mountings, available in numerous varieties and a wide range of sizes, made of base and precious metals: stainless steel, copper, silver-, gold- or rhodium-plated brass, silver, silver-gilt and gold.

Tumble-polished, or *baroque*, stones may be variously shaped, but are often elongated and more pointed at one end than at the other. Such stones lend themselves to mounting in *bell caps*.

A bell cap consists of a small cap, surrounded by a rosette of

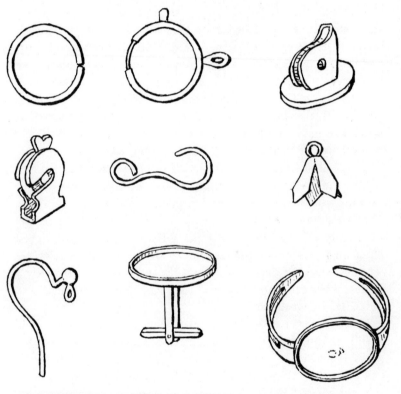

FIG 38 Examples of jeweller's findings: (left to right, from the top) jump ring; bolt ring; fichu hinge; side-opening catch; belt hook; bell cap; ear wire with loop; cufflink; open ring with cabochon mounting

'petals', 'tongues' or 'fingers', with a small ring at the top. The ring serves for suspension, and the 'fingers' are pliable and can be fitted round the thin end of the stone. To obtain a really good, close fit, use may be made of a *burnisher*, which is a tongue-shaped metal or agate tool with a handle, for pressing the 'fingers' against the stone. Once the cap has been fitted to the stone, both the inside of the cap and the part of the stone that goes into it are slightly roughened up with abrasive (eg a not-too-coarse *silicon-carbide stick* —say grade 400) for better adhesion. The next step is to remove all traces of grease and oil from the interfitting parts by washing them, not just in soap and water, but in spirit or carbon tetrachloride. When dry, a little touch of polyester adhesive (eg 'Araldite') is applied to both parts and they are pressed into contact. Any surplus adhesive oozing out between the 'fingers' should be removed, say with a cocktail stick (toothpick), and the cap wiped clean. The bond is then left to set, which will take about twenty-four hours, preferably with the stone standing up cap on top, for instance, in a tray or tin filled with sand or a box with holes in the lid as used for dopsticks (p 88).

Capped stones can be attached to a chain or silver wire by means of split rings, known as *jump rings*, passed through a chain link or over the wire on the one side and through the cap ring on the other. They are supposed to close by their own resilience, but may require in practice a little help from a pair of small pliers. For the best effect the limbs of the ring at the gap should be parted sideways, without widening the ring, and not up and down. Alternatively a double ring of the same design as a key ring only smaller may provide a safer connection.

Medium-sharp tweezers and diagonal cutting pliers may be found useful in handling small objects and cutting silver wire or thin strips of metal.

A number of capped stones attached to a chain will make a necklace or a bracelet, whose loose ends are usually secured to each other with a *bolt ring*, which is a split tubular ring having a gap closed by a spring-loaded arcuate bolt sliding within the open tubular part and equipped with a side projection for easy handling. The bolt ring may be attached to the chain either direct or through a small ring receiving the terminal link. A jump ring of suitable size will provide a connection at the opposite end of the chain. Alternatively a *swivel, snap-hook* or *necklace hook* may be employed.

A sufficiently large and good-looking stone of suitable shape may make a pendant by itself. A bracelet can be made with a flat chain of broad rectangular or square links, in which appropriate stones can be fixed with polyester adhesive, although this plan is better suited to cabochons than baroques. A stone may be drilled, in which case a jump ring or a wire can be passed through the hole. It may also receive an *ear wire* or an *ear screw*, which are among the usual findings.

It will, however, be recalled that drilling hard stones is a difficult job, and there is a way of escape. Instead of a hole, a notch can be cut with a slitting saw in the chosen end of the stone, to receive a jump ring, which is inserted into the notch with its open side, and the notch is then filled with hard-setting plastic cement or adhesive. Since the side view of the notch is blocked by the ring, this will not show at all, unless we look right into the ring, which is not easy, as it will be largely filled by another ring, chain link or wire.

Simple cabochons are even easier to mount than baroque stones, as they are usually opaque or nearly so and have an unpolished flat base, which can be glued straight on to a support plate. Standard brooches, rings, bracelets, cufflinks, etc with flat surfaces for cabochons will be included in any good selection of findings.

Such standardised mountings afford some variety of choice, but this must inevitably be limited. Many of the more elaborate findings tend to be somewhat old-fashioned in style and may not suit every taste. It is also nice to have something more personal, and the only way to achieve this is to design and make a mount of one's own. This requires a few simple tools and some knowledge of metal work.

TOOLS FOR MAKING SIMPLE JEWELLERY

Attractive jewel mounts can be made by the cold method, with possibly a little soldering, using wire and sheet metal.

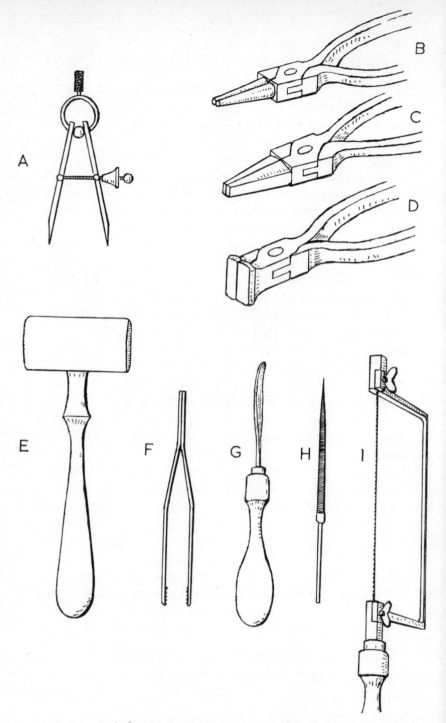

FIG 39 Some tools for making jewellery: A = dividers; B = round-nosed pliers; C = flat-nosed pliers; D = end cutters; E = wooden mallet; F = tweezers; G = burnisher; H = needle file; I = piercing saw

With wire it is all plier work. We need three kinds of small jeweller's pliers: round-nosed, flat-nosed and snipe-nosed, as well as end cutters, to clip off the wire neatly. Although wire lends itself to various interesting designs, these are a little like knitting and not really suitable for mounting gems, except in a wire cage, which is rather like making a virtue of necessity. We may, therefore, pass on to sheet metal, which requires a further set of tools.

The metal sheet may have to be cut, pierced, filed, bent and hammered. The appropriate instruments for these operations are: a piercing saw, a drill, an assortment of files, the already mentioned pliers, and a small wooden mallet. In fact, since the work is very fine, all these tools have to be of a miniature variety. Further adjuncts to this outfit are: a bench pin, fixed to a table top by means of a small G cramp (or C clamp), a scriber (ie a steel stylus for marking the metal), and a pair of accurate dividers for measuring. A small block of hardwood about 1 × 3in in surface measurement may also come in handy as a working base. All of these tools can be obtained from jeweller's outfitters.

The piercing saw is a very fine saw, rather like a fret saw only smaller, exchangeably mounted in a steel frame with a handle. The blade can be tensioned by means of clamp screws at the ends of the frame. Blades are made in various grades, the general rule being that there should be about three teeth to the thickness of the metal sheet to be sawn.

The bench pin is a flat rectangular piece of hardwood with a triangular cut-out at one end. This cut-out may be used to support the saw frame when fitting in a blade, and otherwise serves as an aid in sawing a metal sheet, which is laid flat, clamped or held by hand, on top of the bench pin, the saw blade moving within the cut-out. If the line of the cut is curved the saw is held straight, and the metal sheet is turned slowly instead. If a clear aperture has to be cut inside the sheet, this is first drilled at a suitable point within the aperture, then the blade is threaded through the borehole and fitted into the frame. The sawing is done on the inside of the outline marked with the scriber, and the redundant metal filed away with the square or round side of a *needle file* as the case may be. When the length of the cut exceeds the clear width of the saw frame the blade is twisted with flat-nosed pliers through 90° at both the clamp ends, so that it will saw at right angles to the plane of the frame. The twisting operation must be done very gently, so as not to break the blade.

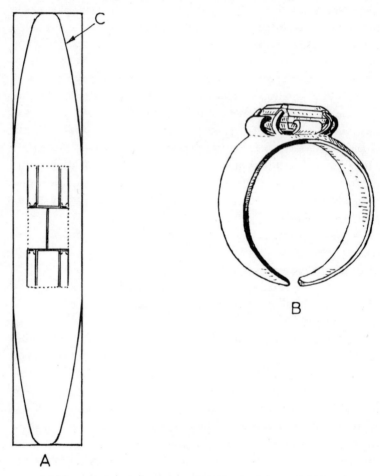

FIG 40 A simple ring cut from a strip of metal as shown in A. Double lines in the middle of the strip indicate cuts. Dotted lines are bending lines. B = complete ring; C = outline of the ring

We will need a half-round half-square needle file, which ends up in a fine point, for delicate work. A larger square, as well as a triangular file will also be found useful.

In drilling, the point at which the hole is to be made should be slightly indented, eg with a fine centre punch, as otherwise the drill bit has a tendency to slip and mark the metal.

Gluing a cabochon to a flat metal surface is a somewhat crude method, but it is adequate for simple rings or bracelets. In the case of facetted stones, double and hollow cabochons, however, the light must be allowed to penetrate under the stone, which is raised above the base of the mount and usually secured by claws bent in to hold it.

I have designed a simple ring (see Fig 40), which can be made from a single strip of sheet metal with the tools and by the methods just described. The broad incurved projections on the long sides of the ring fit under the girdle of the stone and keep it upraised, while the hollow space left by cutting out the projections and claws serves to admit more light to the base of the stone. The transverse clamps and the 45° claws (four in the illustrated example) secure the stone in position against the support of the lateral projections.

The workmanship is fairly obvious. The edges of the ring have to be rounded and smoothed with a file, and the whole polished. The ring is open at the back and so can be adjusted to fit any finger. It may be made of copper and electroplated with silver, gold or rhodium. As usual the article to be plated is connected to the negative terminal and the metal used for plating to the positive terminal (red wire) and both immersed in a solution of a salt of the same metal. The article to be plated and the metal should be chemically clean. Nowadays very thin coatings of rhodium (a highly resistant silvery metal allied to platinum) are applied to jewellery for protection against corrosion. The rhodium film is so thin that it is entirely transparent and undetectable to the eye.

Electroplating with alloys is possible by using appropriate solutions (electrolytes), which is of especial interest in the case of gold. If alloyed in the right proportions to various metals, it yields a whole range of colours: green with silver, blue with iron, violet with aluminium, etc (see p 190). Parts of the plated article can be protected against the deposition of metal by a layer of varnish or wax, and vivid coloured designs can be produced in this way. Colours may also be imparted to the metal by chemical treatment.

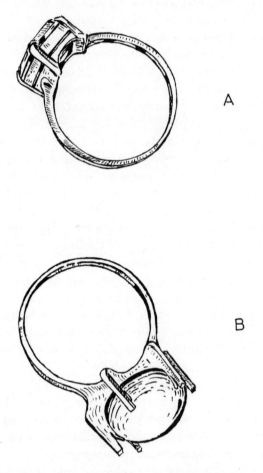

A

B

FIG 41 Examples of rings: A = box mounting for a step-cut gem (designed by Bernard Harrington of the Dundee College of Art); B = spider mounting for a double cabochon (after R. W. Stevens)

To return, however, to my ring, the design can be modified to include two or more stones, or else enlarged into a bracelet, either in one piece or segmental, the segments being joined by hinges or snap rings passed through holes.

Alternatively a clawed plate (oval, circular, square or polygonal) may be soft-soldered to a solid ring by dabbing the parts to be united with flux, hammering a piece of cored solder flat, placing it between them, and heating the whole over a spirit lamp or the like (a piece of cotton-wool imbued with meths will do) until the solder melts. The stone is then mounted on the plate. The sides of the plate may be upwardly flanged, with the claws extending outwards from the flanges. The flanges themselves may be high and slotted to admit light, and the claws bent out and in so as to hold the stone upraised.

These examples are meant to be suggestive rather than exhaustive. There is a whole host of further possibilities on which to exercise our artistic and technical imagination.

LOST WAX METHOD

If we want to enjoy real creative freedom any desired shape can be cast by the lost wax method, which is of venerable antiquity. The essence of the procedure lies in that the envisaged article is first made of wax, then 'invested' in plaster, and when the latter has set the whole is fired, so that the wax melts and flows out through an opening, or sprue hole, provided for this purpose, and the remainder is burnt out. This results in a mould exactly fitting the wax model. The mould is brought to red heat and molten metal is poured in through the sprue hole. When the mould has cooled it is broken up, to reveal the metal casting which is an accurate replica of the original wax model. Anything that can be completely burnt and eliminated, eg a leaf or flower, may be used instead of wax, which opens up various possibilities.

This is the general idea, but carrying it into effect needs some equipment and technical know-how. Special waxes, hard and soft, for carving and moulding are obtainable from dealers. This is small-scale work and requires dainty tools. In fact, it bears some resemblance to the dentist's job, and it has been suggested that discarded dental implements could be employed for making wax models. This may be true, but such implements are expensive to buy and not otherwise easy to obtain. On the other hand, special tools can be purchased from jewellers' outfitters and will last for years. Even this, though, is not really necessary, as a small penknife and a few odd pieces of stout wire or steel knitting needles, suitably filed into points, spatulae, tongues and other handy shapes, will do the trick.

An accurate ring shape may not be easy to mould, but wax rings can be bought ready-made, like findings, or else a metal ring, coated with light machine oil to prevent adhesion, may be repeatedly dipped into a bath of molten wax, the wax layer formed on the ring cut off and used as a basis for our model. A sheet of wax can be cut with a heated knife into strips, which can be rolled into scrolls or similar structures. Wax 'wires' can be squeezed out of an old oil gun or a plastic syringe (so long as the latter is not overheated), and so on.

Once our model has been fully fashioned, it is washed in water and detergent and painted with several successive layers of investment plaster, using a soft water-colour brush, to ensure a good moulding fit. The next stage of investment requires some further equipment, namely the *crucible former* and the *flask*.

The crucible former consists of a flat dish with a vertically raised rim (flange) and a central pierced dome. The dome is hemispherical for *pressure casting* and conical or frustoconical for *centrifugal casting*, of which more presently. The flask bears no resemblance to a bottle, and is a short steel tube, which fits exactly into the rim flange of the crucible former, and must be sufficiently large to accommodate the model and the investment.

A *sprue wire*, which is a short length of wire, very smooth and rounded at the ends, is inserted into the hole at the top of the dome. The crucible former and the wire are coated thinly with light machine oil. The model is supplied with a little wax ball, or *sprue button*, which is impaled upon the sprue wire. The flask is then fitted into

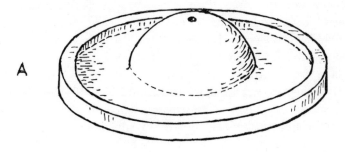

A

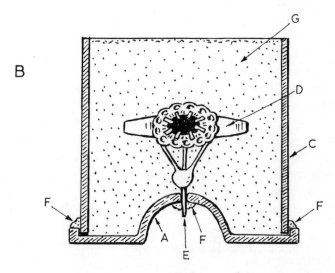

B

FIG 42 Lost wax casting: A = crucible former of the type used in pressure casting. Note the sprue hole at the top of the crucible dome; B = steel flask (C) fitted into crucible former (A) with wax model of a ring (D) with sprue channels and sprue button impaled on sprue wire (E); F = plasticine fillets; G = investment, roughened on top. In partial section (see also page 186)

the crucible former and sealed along its flange with a fillet of plasticine or wax, to prevent leakage. It is ready to be filled with investment plaster, and is vibrated gently during the filling, to expel air bubbles. The investment is allowed to set. The flask is removed from the crucible former and fired, to eliminate the wax, in an enamelling kiln or muffle furnace.

There are two ways of doing this: slow and rapid. The slow way is the more satisfactory, as it eschews possible damage to fine relief.

In the slow method the furnace (or kiln) is preheated to 300°C. The sprue wire is withdrawn, and the flask is placed in the furnace with the crucible (ie the recess formed by the dome) down on supporting legs in a small dish, to allow the melting wax to flow out. The temperature is kept at 300°C for about an hour and then raised slowly to the ultimate 700°C. The burning-out process will take between one and two hours. When the plaster has been burnt white and the sprue hole glows dark red the operation is completed, and the mould is ready for the injection of molten metal.

The metal for the casting, sprue and sprue button is cleansed in acid pickle and melted. If old scrap is used, it must be free from solder, and it is advisable to add one half of fresh material. The amount required can be judged by immersing the model in a graduated beaker filled with water and noting how much water it displaces. It is always better to take a little more metal than is needed to fill the volume thus estimated—just in case.

For obtaining a good casting the metal must be forced to enter every part of the mould, which must be completely filled. There are various methods of ensuring this, but we will consider only the two simplest ones.

The Solbrig method relies on steam pressure. In this the hot mould with molten metal is placed with the crucible up upon an asbestos support, and a wet asbestos pad is rammed into the crucible by means of a disc fixed to a long lever anchored at one end. As the water in the pad turns to steam, this generates considerable pressure in the sprue hole and forces the melt into the mould. Alternatively air pressure may be employed (see plate, p 186).

In the centrifugal method the flask is placed in a small bucket which is fixed to a chain with a handle. The bucket with the flask, containing the mould and molten metal, is swung round on the chain, and the centrifugal force of rotation presses the metal into the mould. The method is not without its dangers, and sufficient skill in swinging the bucket must be acquired before this can be attempted with molten metal.

The following short table may be of some assistance:

Red heat				500–600°C
White heat				1,500–1,800°C
Melting point of			silver	961°C
,,	,,	,,	brass	800–1000°C
,,	,,	,,	German silver	1,050°C
,,	,,	,,	gold	1,063°C
,,	,,	,,	rhodium	1,960°C

Alloys generally have a lower melting point than their constituent pure metals. The listed metals, except for rhodium, can be melted in the heat of a blowlamp or a bunsen burner. Rhodium would require an oxy-hydrogen torch and is correspondingly difficult to handle.

The metal is preheated to red heat in a reducing (white or yellow) flame, placed in the mould crucible and further heated in the reducing flame until it melts and begins to spin. A pinch of borax will expedite the process.

When the casting operation has been completed, we must wait till the sprue button solidifies and turns black. At this point the mould is plunged into water and rapidly chilled, which makes the plaster brittle and easy to remove.

This is a simplified account of the lost wax method, and the reader is referred to specialised works for fuller particulars.

MISCELLANEOUS
INFORMATION

January	garnet	July	ruby or onyx
February	amethyst	August	sardonyx
March	bloodstone or jasper	September	olivine
April	diamond or sapphire	October	opal or beryl
May	emerald or carnelian	November	topaz
June	agate or chalcedony	December	turquoise or ruby

LANGUAGE OF GEMS

Magical properties were ascribed to gems in antiquity, and they have come to symbolise the corresponding emotions or intentions, and so have been used to convey messages as presents.

Agate—insures health, long life and prosperity
Amethyst—prevents violent passions (and drunkenness)
Beryl—symbolises eternal youth and happiness
Bloodstone—denotes steadfast affection, courage and wisdom
Carnelian—a charm against misfortune
Cats-eye—warns against danger and trouble
Chalcedony—drives away sadness
Diamond—signifies purity, maintains peace
Emerald—exposes false friends and ensures true love
Garnet—symbolises constancy and fidelity
Jasper—wisdom and courage

Page 185 (*right*) Viking VT-35 Vibra-Sonic Tumbler (American) by Geode Industries Inc, of New London, Iowa. This is a very large vibratory tumbler with a single hopper (drum) taking up to 35lb load, fitted out for Gemrocks Ltd with a British-made $\frac{1}{4}$ HP 230 V 50 cycle motor. It has a micro-dial control to suit any type of load, a hopper of cast aluminium with vinyl lining and sealed ball bearings with urethane drive transmission; (*below*) Viking VT-6 Rotary Tumbler. The polyvinyl barrel on angled shaft is shaped to lift the load in addition to rotation, altering the position of the whole mass six times per revolution

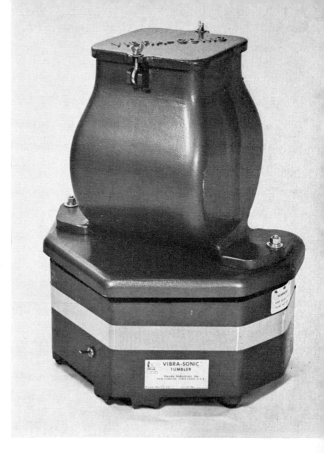

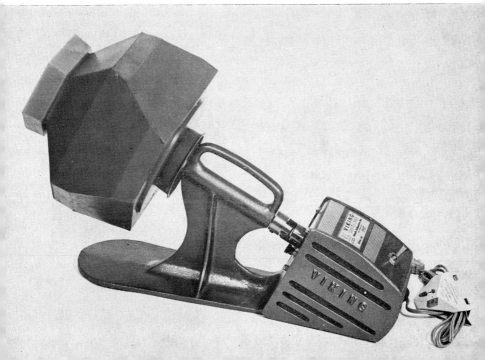

Page 186 (*above*) Gemrocks (British) Varispeed Tumbler. This has no belts or pulleys, but an inbuilt continuous-duty motor with frictional drive. A rubber-sealed barrel with venting valve is supported on short rollers and the operational parts are enclosed in a ventilated metal box; (*below*) lost wax casting outfit, comprising carving stand with five ring mandrels (sizes L, M, O, Q and S—*see* p 189), brass ring measuring stick, spirit lamp, carving and modelling tools and materials, investment mixing bowl, air-pressure casting kit with investment flasks and crucible former, asbestos gloves, etc

Moonstone—brings good luck
Onyx—ensures conjugal fidelity
Opal—a stone of ill-omen, portending loss, injury or madness
Pearl—signifies purity and innocence
Peridot (olivine)—dispels evil passions and melancholy
Ruby—discovers poison, corrects the evils of false friendship
Sapphire—denotes repentance, breaks spells
Sardonyx—a symbol of married happiness
Topaz—signifies fidelity and friendship; a charm against bad dreams
Turquoise—symbol of love and success

It will be observed that most gemstones are free from such connotations, and those listed are associated with their traditional colours: garnet is red, beryl—golden, jasper—red, sapphire—blue, and topaz—yellow.

WEIGHTS OF GEMS AND PRECIOUS METALS

Gems are weighed in metric carats or Troy ounces

1 carat = 2g = 3·086 grains (Troy) = 0·007oz (Avoirdupois)

1oz (Troy) = 20dwt = 480 grains = 155·54 carats

1oz (Avoirdupois) = 16 drachms = $437\frac{1}{2}$ grains = 141·76 carats = 0·91146oz (Troy) = 28·35g

In weighing pearls the term grain denotes the weight of $\frac{1}{4}$ carat

The word carat is also used to describe the proportion by weight of the precious metal in an alloy. In this case carat does not correspond to any fixed weight, but to $\frac{1}{24}$ of the total weight. 18-carat gold contains $\frac{18}{24}$ of gold by weight; pure gold is 24 carat.

CIRCLE AND SPHERE

	Number	Logarithm
π =	3·1416	0·4971
$\frac{4}{3}\pi$ =	4·1888	0·6221

Circle: circumference $= 2\pi r$, area $= \pi r^2$, where r is the radius ($\frac{1}{2}$ of the diameter)

Flat ring of width a and outer radius r: area $= 2\pi ar - \pi a^2$

Upright ring of width a and radius r: strip area $= 2\pi ar$

Sphere: surface $= 4\pi r^2$, volume $= \frac{4}{3}\pi r^3$

CONVERSION OF WEIGHTS AND MEASURES

	Reciprocal
1 grain $= 0\cdot064789$g	$15\cdot4324$ (grains $= 1$g)
1dwt $= 1\cdot55518$g	$0\cdot64301$
1oz Troy $= 31\cdot1035$g	$0\cdot032151$
1oz Av $= 28\cdot3495$g	$0\cdot035274$
1oz Troy $= 1\cdot09716$oz Av	$0\cdot911458$
1oz Av $= 437\cdot0$ grains	$0\cdot0022857$
1oz Troy $= 480\cdot0$ grains	$0\cdot0020833$
1lb Av $= 0\cdot453524$kg	$2\cdot20462$
1lb Av $= 7000\cdot0$ grains	$0\cdot000143$
1in $= 254$mm ($2\cdot54$cm)	$0\cdot03937$
1in^2 $= 645\cdot16$mm^2	$0\cdot00155$
1in^3 $= 16\cdot3871$cm^3 (cc)	$0\cdot061024$
1fl oz (UK) $= 28\cdot4$ml or cc	$0\cdot03521$
100cc $= 3\cdot521$oz UK $= 3\cdot81$fl oz US	
1pt (UK) $= 568\cdot25$cc $= 0\cdot56825$l	$1\cdot7600$
1qt (UK) $= 1136\cdot5$cc $= 1\cdot1365$l	$0\cdot8800$
1Imp gal (UK) $= 4\cdot546$l	$0\cdot2200$
1Imp gal $= 277.42$in^3	$0\cdot003605$
1US gal $= 231\cdot00$in^3	$0\cdot004329$
1Imp gal $= 6/5$US gal	$5/6$
1pt (US) $= 473\cdot1$cc $= 0\cdot4731$l	$1\cdot0560$
1qt (US) $= 946\cdot3$cc $= 0\cdot9463$l	$0\cdot5280$

RING SIZES

British standard ring sizes are indicated by the capital letters of the alphabet with half-sizes in between, from A and A$\frac{1}{2}$ to Z and Z$\frac{1}{2}$, which covers a range from 0·475in to 0·870in in inner diameter in 52 grades, each half-step corresponding to between 0·007in and 0·008in.

In the *American* system there are 25 half-sizes, numbered from 1 to 13 and ranging from the inner diameter of 0·486in to 0·875in, the half-size step being approximately 0·016in.

In the *European Continental* system there are 32 sizes, numbered from 32 to 69, which correspond to inner diameters of 0·4762in and 0·8647in respectively, the step between the divisions being 0·0125in to 0·0126in. It will be seen that the divisions in this system fit in between those of the other two.

METAL GAUGES

Metal sheet and wire are graded and assigned numbers according to thickness or gauge. The gauge numbers have to be specified in ordering materials from suppliers. Sheet thicknesses are standardised in the *Birmingham Metal* or *Shakespeare Gauge*, which has 40 divisions, 1 corresponding to the thickness of 0·0085in = 0·216mm and 40 to 0·300in = 7·620mm. The wire diameters run in the opposite direction. The *British Standard Wire Gauge* extends to 35 grades, where 1 is the same as 40 for metal sheet, and 35 is somewhat less than 1 for sheet, namely 0·0084in = 0·213mm. The American *Brown and Sharpe Wire Gauge* is slightly different from the British and has 31 divisions, in which the thickest 1 is 0·289in = 7·341mm, and the thinnest 31 is somewhat below the British 34 and measures 0·0089in = 0·228mm. The American No. 30 coincides with the British No. 33, and 25 with 24, and there are other coincidences along the scale. None of these scales is consistently progressive, inasmuch as the difference between the successive grades is only approximately constant.

COLOURS OF GOLD ALLOYS, ETC

As mentioned on p 177, gold alloys can assume every colour of the rainbow depending on composition. Here are some examples of 18-carat, or 75 per cent pure, gold alloys:

Gold alloyed with	Colour
25 % copper	red gold
22·25 % silver, 2·75 % copper	rose gold
20 % copper, 5 % silver	light red
15 % silver, 10 % copper	'pearl'
16·75 % silver, 8·25 % copper	pale yellow
15·5 % copper, 9·5 % silver	deep yellow
17 % white iron, 8 % copper	grey
25 % pure white iron	blue
23 % silver, 2 % cadmium	light green
20 % silver, 5 % copper	medium green
15 % silver, 6 % copper, 4 % cadmium	deep green
25 % silver	full green
18·75 % palladium, 6·25 % silver	brown
25 % palladium	hard, white
12 % nickel, 10 % palladium, 4 % zinc, 4 % cadmium	soft, white
28 % aluminium, 15 % thorium, 0·5 % tin	purple

Electrum is an alloy of gold and silver containing between 55 and 88 per cent of fine gold. In rolled gold a layer of gold alloy is superimposed by welding and rolling on to a sheet of base metal or silver. In gold plate a thin layer of fine gold is deposited electrolytically on base metal. Like gold, pure silver is a little too soft for most applications, so that it is usually stiffened with an admixture of copper or other metals, but nickel silver is an alloy of nickel, copper and zinc containing no silver at all. German silver is any similar alloy, containing 25–50 per cent of copper, 10–35 per cent of zinc, and 3–35 per cent of nickel.

CRITICAL ANGLE (WITH REFERENCE TO P 35 AND FIGS 8 AND 9)

The diagram (Fig 8) remains correct if the direction in which the light moves is reversed, the beam of light passing from the stone into air. The refractive index of the stone RI $= \dfrac{\sin \alpha}{\sin \beta}$, and the critical angle corresponds to the situation where $\alpha = 90°$. The value of β will then be that of the critical angle.

Sin $90° = 1$, so that RI $= \dfrac{1}{\sin \beta} = \operatorname{cosec} \beta$. Most mathematical tables give natural cosecants, and the critical angle is the angle whose cosecant has the numerical value of the RI.

The RI of diamond is 2·42, which is the cosecant of 24° 21′; the RI of quartz is 1·55, yielding a critical angle of 40° 8′, and so on.

CALCULATING THE ANGLE OF REFRACTION (WITH REFERENCE TO P 107)

We may call the angle in air α, which may be one of incidence or refraction, for, as stated in the preceding section, the refraction diagram can always be viewed upside down. If now β be the angle in the stone we shall have:

$$\dfrac{\sin \alpha}{\sin \beta} = \text{RI, or } \sin \alpha = \text{RI} \cdot \sin \beta, \text{ and } \sin \beta = \dfrac{\sin \alpha}{\text{RI}}.$$

To avoid multiplication and division, we may use logarithmic sines instead, and it will then be:

$$\log \sin \alpha = \log \text{RI} + \log \sin \beta, \text{ and}$$
$$\log \sin \beta = \log \sin \alpha - \log \text{RI}$$

To take a concrete example:

Quartz: RI $= 1·54$; critical angle $= 40° 30′$
$\alpha = 32°$; $\beta = ?$
$\log \sin 32° = \bar{1}·7242$; $\log 1·54 = 0·1875$
$\log \sin \beta = \bar{1}·7242 - 0·1875 = \bar{1}·5367$
$\beta = 21° 7′$

Such four-figure accuracy is far in excess of the practical requirements, as an angle of 7' can neither be read off an ordinary protractor nor set on a facetting head with any pretension to precision;
the best we can hope for is 10', or $\frac{1}{6}$ of a degree of arc.

SUPPLIERS OF LAPIDARY AND JEWELLERY MAKING EQUIPMENT AND ROUGH GEMSTONE MATERIAL

The following lists are as exhaustive as possible, but it will be appreciated that a halt must be called somewhere, and the omission of any particular firm arises solely from the considerations of space. (L) after the address indicates a supplier of lapidary equipment; (J) stands similarly for jewellery making accessories; and (M) refers to minerals and gemstones. In so extensive a list it is difficult to discriminate between manufacturers, wholesalers and retailers, the more so as many firms operate in all these capacities simultaneously.

UNITED KINGDOM

Ammonite Ltd, Llandow Industrial Estate, Cowbridge, Glamorganshire (JLM)

Art and Crafts Unlimited, 49 Shelton St, London WC2 (JLM)

Avon Gems, Strathavon Boon St, Eckington, nr Pershore, Worcestershire (JM)

M. L. Beach (Products) Ltd, 41 Church St, Twickenham, Middlesex and 7 Kings Parade, Ditching Rd, Brighton, Sussex (JLM)

Bede-Brown (Metalcraft), 1 Hereford Way, Fellgate, Jarrow, Co. Durham (J)

Bezalel Gems Co., New House, 67–8 Hatton Garden, London EC1 (M)

Nancy Black, Albany St, Oban, Argyll (JLM)

Brydon, 18 Wordsworth Rd, Colne, Lancashire (JLM)

G. & B. Butler, 18B The Pantiles, Tunbridge Wells, Kent (JM)

Caverswall Minerals, The Dams, Caverswall, Stoke-on-Trent, Staffordshire (JLM)

Charles Cooper (H. G.) Ltd, Wall House, 12 Hatton Wall, Hatton Garden, London EC1 (J)

Edith Constable, 63 Coronation Drive, Frizington, Cumberland (M)

Craftorama (Wholesale) Co., 14 Endell St., London WC2 (J)

Fife Stone Craft, 3 Edison House, Fullerton Rd, Glenrothes, Fifeshire (JLM)

Fisher Gems and Minerals, 43 Hazelwood Rd, Northamptonshire (M)

Gemlines, 10 Victoria Crescent, London SW19 (M)

'Gemma', 494 Nottingham Rd, Chaddesdem, Derbyshire (JLM)

Geobright and the Glass Man, 28 Queens Rd, Brighton, Sussex (JLM)

Gemrocks Ltd, Halton House, 20–3 Holborn, London EC1 (JLM)

Gemset, 8 Manor St, Bridlington, Yorkshire (JLM)

Gemset of Broadstairs Ltd, 31 Albion St, Broadstairs, Kent (JLM)

Gemstones, 35 Princes Ave, Hull, Yorkshire, and
9 Bapton Lane, Exmouth, Devon (JLM)

Glenjoy Lapidary Supplies, 89 Westgate, Wakefield, Yorkshire (JLM)

E. Gray & Son, Grayson House, 12–14–16 Clerkenwell Rd, London EC1 (J)

H. & T. Gems, 31 Rosebury Rd, Hartlepool, Co. Durham (JLM)

Highland Line, The Old Stables, Achnasheen, Ross-shire (M)

Hillside Gems, Terminus Shopping Centre (A38), Wylde Green, Sutton Coldfield, Staffordshire (JLM)

Hoben Davis Ltd, Spencroft Rd, Newcastle-under-Lyme, Staffordshire (J)

R. Holt & Co. Ltd, 92 Hatton Garden, London EC1 (JM)

Howard Minerals Ltd, 27 Heddon St, London W1 (JLM)

A. & D. Hughes Ltd, Popes Lane, Oldbury, Warley, Worcestershire (JLM)

International Craft, PO Box 73, Hemel Hempstead, Hertfordshire (JLM)

Hirsh Jacobson Merchandising Co. Ltd, 91 Marylebone High St, London W1 (JLM)

Johnson Matthey & Co. Ltd, Victoria St, Birmingham 1 (J)

E. P. Joseph Ltd, 70–1 New Bond St, London W1 (M)

Kernowcraft Rocks & Gems, 68 Highertown, Truro, Cornwall (JLM)

Keystones, 1 Local Board Rd, Watford, Hertfordshire (LM)

Kristalap Ltd, 13–14 Great Sutton St, London EC1 (L)

Lakeland Rock Shop, Pack Horse Court, Keswick, Cumberland (M)

R. Lane, 'The Haven', Danes Rd, Awbridge, Romsey, Hampshire (JLM)

Lapidary Abrasives, 14 Market St, Altrincham, Cheshire (L)

Lapidary Wholesale Supply Co., 46 Walmsley St, Hull, Yorkshire (L)

Little Rocks, 36 Oakwood Ave, Cardiff, Glamorganshire (JM)

Love-Rocks, 56–8 North St, Bedminster, Bristol (M)

Lythe Minerals, 36 Oxford St, Leicester (M)

Manchester Minerals, 33 School Lane, Heaton Chapel, Stockport, Cheshire (JLM)

A. Massie & Son, 158 Burgoyne Rd, Sheffield 8, Yorkshire (JLM)

Mineral Imports, 72 Netheravon Rd, London W4 (M)

Mineralcraft, D. M. Naylor, 1 The Knoll, Crown Hill, Rayleigh, Essex (M)

Minerals & Gemstones (Penzance), Trewellard Rd, Pendeen, nr Penzance, Cornwall (LM)

Minerocks, Hampstead Antique Emporium, 12 Heath St, London NW3 (JLM)

Natural Gems Ltd, Kingsbury Square, Aylesbury, Buckinghamshire (J)

Norgems, 4 Front St, Sandbach, Cheshire (JLM)

A. T. Nunn, 5 Pool Valley, Brighton, Sussex (M?)

Opie Gems, 13 Gilbert Close, Hempstead, Gillingham, Kent (JLM)

Kenneth Parkinson, 11 Fitzroy St, Hull, Yorkshire (JLM)

R. F. D. Parkinson & Co. Ltd, Doulting, Shepton Mallet, Somerset (M)

Pebblegems, 51 King James Ave, Cuffley, Potters Bar, Hertfordshire, and 88A Wallis Rd, London E9 (JLM)

Lionel Pepper, 4A Abbeville Rd, London SW4 (J)

PMR Lapidary Equipment & Supplies, Smithy House, Atholl Rd, Pitlochry, Perthshire (JLM)

Rocks and Minerals, 4 Moorcourt Drive, Cheltenham, Gloucestershire (M)

Rough & Tumble Ltd, 3 Tyne St, North Shields, Northumberland (JLM)

Scotrocks Partners, 196 W Princes St, Helensburgh, Dunbartonshire, and 48 Park Rd, Glasgow C4, and 122 Rose St, South Lane, Edinburgh (JLM)

J. Simble & Sons, Dept 76, Queens Rd, Watford, Hertfordshire (L)

Stones & Settings, 54 Main St, Prestwick, Ayrshire, and 45 Main St, Ayr (JM)

Strathclyde Studio, Scilly Banks, Whitehaven, Cumberland (JLM)

Sutherland Gem Cutters, Achmelvich by Lairg, Sutherland (?)

The Rock Shop, 2 Sidon Place, Havre des Pas, Jersey, Channel Islands (M)

The Rockhound Shop, The White House, Front St, Newbiggin-by-Sea, Northumberland (JLM)

The Stone Corner, 21 High St, Hastings, Sussex (JLM)

Tideswell Dale Rock Shop, Tideswell, Derbyshire (M?)

Timgems, The Old Shop, Ludham, Great Yarmouth, Norfolk (JLM)

Tor Minerals, 30 Marshall Ave, Wadebridge, Cornwall (JLM)

Tudor Amethyst, 24 West St, Exeter, Devon (JLM)

Tumble Kraft, 10 High St, Rochester, Kent (JM)

Wessex Gems and Crafts, Longacre, Down Rd, South Wonstron, Winchester, Hampshire (JLM)

Wessex Impex Ltd, Gemini, Lanham Lane, Winchester, Hampshire (JLM)

Whithear Lapidary Co., 35 Ballards Lane, London N3 (L)

AUSTRALIA AND NEW ZEALAND

Antipodean Gemrock, PO Box 84, Killara, New South Wales (M)

Australian Gem Trading Co., 294 Little Collins St, Melbourne (M)

Campbell's Gemstones Pty Ltd, 800 Nepean Highway, Morabbin, Melbourne 3189 (M?)

Commercial Gem and Lapidary Distributors Pty Ltd, 6 Butler St, Doveton 3177, Victoria (JLM)

Ezycut Tool Co. Pty Ltd, 71 White St, Mordialloc, Victoria 3195 (L)

Goodland Enterprises, PO Box 6, Nobby's Beach, Queensland (M?)

Kovac's Gems and Minerals Pty Ltd, 120–2 Commercial Rd, Frahran, Melbourne 3181 (M)

Minex Lapidary Supplies Pty Ltd, 206 Russell St, Melbourne 3000 (JLM)

Queensland Opal Cutters, PO Box 154, Gladstone, Queensland 4680 (M)

Daryl Roder, Box 77, The Post Office, The Opal Fields, Andamooka, Southern Australia (M)

D. F. Roder, Box 85, Cowandilla, Adelaide, Southern Australia 5033 (M)

Rytime Robilt Pty Ltd, 218 Bay Rd, Sandringham, Victoria 3191 (L)

Space Stones, Chillingollah PO, Victoria 3535 (M)

Spring Enterprises (Aust) Pty Ltd, Box 372, PO, Surfers Paradise, Queensland 4217 (M?)

Superior Gemstones Pty Ltd, 42–4 Treacy St, Hurtsville, New South Wales (M?)

Trans-Australia Gems Exports, 12–34 Diamond Bay Rd, Vaucluse 2030, Sydney (M)

P. Wright, 4 Quintus Terrace, Dover Gardens, Southern Australia 5048 (M?)

CANADA

Apex Minerals and Lapidary, Box 4731, Station C, Vancouver, British Columbia (JLM)

Canadian Gems & Minerals Ltd, Drawer 730, Kirkland Lake, Ontario (M)

Charbonneau's Lapidary Services, 4020 Bow Trail SW, Calgary, Alberta (JLM)

Kel Findings, 455 West Ave, Kelowna, British Columbia (JLM)

Lee's Jades and Opals, 3563 232nd St, RR 3, Langley, British Columbia (M)

Marshall's Lapidary Co. Ltd, 2025 West 41st Ave, Vancouver, British Columbia (L)

New World Jade Ltd, 1696 Centre St North, Calgary 41, Alberta (M)
Rock & Lapidary Ltd, 1603 Centre St North, Calgary, Alberta (JLM)
Village Rock Shop, Shakespeare, Ontario (M?)
Williams-Hildas, 2591 Yonge St, Toronto (?)

INDIA

V. P. Bhatia, 56 Rajendra Nagar, Agra 1 (M)
Keshaval Mohanlal E. & Sons, 81 Marine Drive, Bombay 2 (M)
Mithabazar Trading Corp, Jullundur City (M)
Parasmani K. Trading Co., 1312 Prasadchambers, Opera House, Bombay 4 (M)
Pitemberdass Mohanlal & Sons, 4 Mandlik Rd, Colaba, Bombay 1 (M)
Ratashi Bhawanji, 99 'Rajgor Chambers', 5th Floor, Room 502, Masjid Siding Rd, Bombay 400009 (M)
S. Tyebjee 31, Wodehouse Rd, Bombay (M)

UNITED STATES OF AMERICA

Aleta's Rock Shop, 1515 Plainfiled NE, Grand Rapids, Michigan (M)
Allen Lapidary Equipment Manufacturing Co., PO Box 75411, Oklahoma City, Oklahoma 73107 (L)
Alpha Faceting Supply, Dept D, Box 2133, Bremerton, Washington 98310 (JLM)
Alta Industries, 918 W Norwich Ave, Fresno, California 93705 (L)
American Gems Inc, Hiddenite, North Carolina 28636(EM) (M)
American Gems and Minerals, PO Box 903, Miami, Florida 33148 (M)
Arlene Handley Rock Hobby Supplies, 800 NW 72nd Way, Vancouver, Washington 98665 (M)
Arrow Profile Co., PO Box 38, St Clair Shores, Michigan 48080 (L)
Art House, PO Box 22066, Cleveland, Ohio 44122 (M)
Australian Imports, 3684 Fairmount Ave, San Diego, California 92105 (M)
B. & I. Manufacturing, Dept L, Box 146, Adrian, Michigan 49221 (L)
Barnard's, 4724 Broadway, Kansas City, Missouri 64112 (LM)

Beacon Star, Rothsay, Minnesota 56579 (L)

Bergsten Jade Co., Box 2381, Castro Valley, California 94546 (M)

Dorothy Blake, 1700 S Bedford St, Los Angeles, California 90035 (L)

California Crafts Supply, 1419 N Central Part Ave, Anaheim, California 92802 (JL)

Colbaugh's Manufacturing Co., Chloride Star Rt 93, Box 210, Kingman, Arizona, 8641 (L)

Commercial Mineral Corp, 22 W 48th St, New York, NY 10036 (M)

Covington, Box 35, Redlands L, California 92373 (L)

Crestmark Manufacturing Co. Inc, 17–25 Camden St, Peterson, NJ 07503 (J)

Diamond-PRO Unlimited, PO Box 25, Monterey Park, California 91754 (L)

DW Products Co., Box R, Escondido, California 92025 (L)

Exacta, Box 5072, Dept J, Garden Grove, California 92641 (L)

Frances Paul Crafts, 3033 La Madera Ave, El Monte, California 91732 (L)

Sam Frost, The Mayard Building, 175 Canada St, Lake George, New York (L)

Gem-o-rama, 64 Poole Circle (Dept 3), Holbrook, Massachusetts 02343 (L)

Gem-Tec Diamond Tool Co., PO Box 4454, Inglewood, California 9039 (L)

Gem World Lapidary Rock Shop, 847 Lee St SW, Atlanta, Georgia 30310 (JLM)

Geode Industries, 106–8 W Main, US Highway 34, New London, Iowa 52645 (L)

Goodnow Gems USA, 3608 Sunlite, Amarillo, Texas 79109 (M)

Gordon's Gems & Minerals, PO Box 4073, 1741 Cherry, Long Beach, California 90804 (M)

Great Western Equipment Co., 3444 Main St, Chula Vista, California 92011 (L)

Grieger's Inc, Dept 41, 1633 E Walnut St, Pasadena, California 91109 (JLM)

Highland Park Manufacturing, 12600 Chadron Ave, Hawthorne, California 90250 (L)

W. D. Hudson Jr, 4692 E Ponce de Leon Ave, Stone Mountain, Georgia 30083 (M)

India Jewelry & Gifts, Inc, 18 W 45th St, New York, NY 10036 (M)

International Import Co., 2420 Fawn Ridge Drive, Stone Mountain, Georgia 30083 (M)

Jade World, 7960 Uva Drive, Redwood Valley, California 95470 (M)

Jewelcraft, 4959 York Blvd, Los Angeles, California 90042 (JL)

Lee Lapidaries, 3425 W 117th St, Cleveland, Ohio 4411 (L)

Lovelace Rock & Mineral Shop, 2610 Armory Rd, Wichita Falls, Texas 76302 (M)

Magic Circle Corp, 714 10th Ave East, Seattle, Washington 98122 (J)

A. D. McBurney, 1610 Victory Blvd, Glendale, California 91201 (L)

MDR Manufacturing Co. Inc, 4853 J W R Jefferson Blvd, Los Angeles, California 90016 (L)

Miller Manufacturing Inc, 101 W Main, Waterville, Minnesota 56096 (L)

MK Diamond Products, 12600 Chadron Ave, Hawthorne, California 90250 (L)

Mohave Industries, 3770 Hearne Ave, Kingman, Arizona 86401 (L)

Mueller's, 100 E Camelback, Phoenix, Arizona 85014 (M)

Murray American Corp, 15 Commerce St, Chatham, New Jersey 07928 (M)

Myer's Pebble Palace, 6139 Mission St, Daly City, California 94016 (JLM)

Myron Toback Inc, 23 W 47th St, New York, NY 10036 (L)

Nogales Manufacturing Co., Box 1745, Nogales, Arizona 85621 (L)

Oceanside Gem Imports Inc, Box 222, 426 Marion St, Oceanside, New York 1157 (M)

Oregon Gem Stones, 5844 SW 33rd Place, Portland, Oregon 97219 (M)

Parser Mineral Corp, Box 2076, Danbury, Connecticut 06810 (M)

Plummer's Minerals, 4720 Point Lama Ave, Ocean Beach Area, San Diego, California 92107 (M)

Prismatic Instruments, 3507 W Lacrosse, Spokane, Washington 99205 (L)

Rainbow Rock Shop, 3844 Upton Ave, Toledo, Ohio (M)

Raytech Industries Inc, River Rd, PO Box 84A, Stafford Springs, Connecticut 06076 (L)

Rock Shop, York River Mining Co., 9618 Parkman Rd, Windham, Ohio (M)

Rock's Lapidary Equipment, PO Box 10075, San Antonio, Texas 78210 (L)

Shipley's Mineral House, Gem Village, Bayfield 1, Colorado 81122 (L)

Sinkansas Diamond Products, PO Box 201, La Jolla, California 92037 (L)

Arnita B. Sprague, PO Box 1221, Apache Junction, Arizona 85220 (M)

Gerald Staller, Route 3, Box 167, Port Atkinson, Wisconsin 53538 (M)

Stanley Lapidary Products, 503-F SO Grand Ave, Santa Ana, California 92705 (L)

Star Diamond Industries Inc, 1421 W 240 St, Harbor City, California 90710 (L)

Starlite Rock Shop, 5413 Starlite Rd, Dunuque, Iowa 52001 (M)

Technical Specialities International Inc, 487 Elliot Ave West, Seattle, Washington 98119 (JL)

Technicraft Lapidaries Corp, 2248 Broadway, New York, New York 10024 (JLM)

The Gem Guild, Box 713, Mill Valley, California 94941 (M)

The House of Manhattan, PO Box 421-B, Manhattan Beach, California 90266 (L)

The Newall Manufacturing Co., 139 North Wabash Ave, Chicago, Illinois 60602 (J)

The Treasure Chest, PO Box 54, Rt 40 Havre de Grace, Maryland 21078 (M)

Timberline Lake Rock & Gem Shop, US Hi-way 65, Box 188, Lincoln, Missouri 85338 (M)

United Abrasive Inc, 910 Brown St, Norway, Michigan 49870 (L)
Universal Gems & Minerals Inc, 5951 Griems Ct, El Paso, Texas 79905 (M)
G. Weidinger, PO Box 5, Cape Coral, Florida 33904 (LM)
Weidinger Inc, PO Box 39, Matteson, Illinois 60443 (L)
World Wide Gems, 146 Rose St, Kalamazoo, Michigan 49006 (M)

ELSEWHERE (GEMS AND MINERALS ONLY)

B.E.R.K., 547 Cameron St, Bailey's Muckleneuk, Pretoria, South Africa
Frank & Co., PO Box 58428, Taipei, Taiwan (Formosa)
Gebr Kuhn, 6581 Moerschied/Idar-Oberstein, West Germany
Hong Kong Gems Ltd, 325 Man Yee Building, Hong Kong
W. Martin Blum & Cia Ltda, PO Box 1974, Rua 24 de Maio 276, São Paolo, Brazil
Alberto Ramirez, GLZ, 707 Ninos Heroes Ave, Tijuana, Mexico
'Sinbad Carey', PO Box 2, Kalk Bay, Cape, South Africa

BIBLIOGRAPHY

LAPIDARY WORK

Balej, Ronald J. *Tumbler's Guide*, Minnesota Lapidary Supplies Inc, Minneapolis (1963)

Balej, Ronald J. *Gemcutter's Guide*, Minnesota Lapidary Supplies Inc, Minneapolis (1963)

Barber, Janet. *Pebbles as a Hobby*, Pelham Books, London (1972)

Cooper, Lyn and Ray. *New Zealand Gemstones*, A.H. & A.W. Reed, Wellington, Auckland and Sydney (1969)

Dake, H. C. *The Art of Gem Cutting*, Gembooks, Mentone, California

Hutton, Helen. *Practical Gemstone Craft*, Studio Vista, London (1972)

Jerrard, R. A. *The Amateur Jeweller*, D. B. Barton (1972)

Quick, Leland and Leiper, Hugh. *Gemcraft*, Pitman, London (1967)

Scarfe, Herbert. *Collecting and Polishing Stones*, Batsford, London (1971)

Scarfe, Herbert. *Cutting and Setting Stones*, Batsford, London (1972)

Sinkansas, John. *Gem Cutting—A Lapidary Manual*, Van Nostrand, New York (1963)

Sperisen, Francis J. *The Art of the Lapidary*, Bruce Publishing Co., Milwaukee (1950)

Vargas, Glenn and Martha. *Faceting for Amateurs*, Desert Printers, Palm Desert, California (1969)

Wainwright, John. *Discovering Lapidary Work*, Mills & Boon, London (1971)

MAKING JEWELLERY

Blakemore, Kenneth. *Retail Jeweller's Guide*, Iliffe Press, London (1969)

Choate, Sharr and May, B. C. *Creative Gold and Silversmithing*, Allen & Unwin, London (1971)

Choate, Sharr. *Creative Casting*, Allen & Unwin, London (1967)

Crawford, John. *Introducing Jewellery Making*, Batsford, London (1969)

Edwards, K. and Graham Davies. *Lost Wax Air Pressure Casting*, Mills & Boon, London (1971)

Geoffroy-Dechaume, C. *Simple Craft Jewellery*, Faber, London (1954)

Gooden, R. and Popham, P. *Silversmithing*, London/New York (1971)

Hughes, Graham. *Modern Jewellery*, Studio Books, London (1964)

Lammer, Jutta. *Make Your Own Enamels*, Batsford, London (1968)

Lammer, Jutta. *Make Your Own Custom Jewellery*, Batsford, London (1970)

Maryon, H. *Metalwork and Enamelling*, Chapman & Hall, London (1954)

Neumann, Robert von. *Design and Creation in Jewellery*, Pitman, London (1968)

Richie, Carson I. A. *Carving Shells and Cameos*, Barker, London (1970)

Sopcak, J. E. *Handbook of Lost Wax or Investment Casting*, Gembooks, Mentone, California (1969)

Stevens, R. W. *Simple Jewelry*, Studio Vista, London (1966); and Watson-Guptill Publications, New York (1966)

Weiner, Louis. *Hand-made Jewellery*, Van Nostrand, New York

Wilson, Harry. *Silverwork and Jewellery*, Pitman, London (1966)

MINERALOGY AND GEMMOLOGY

Anderson, B. W. *Gem Testing*, Temple Press, London (1958)

Blakemore, K. and Andrews, G. *Collecting Gems and Ornamental Stones*, Foyle, London (1967)

Börner, R. *Minerals, Rocks and Gemstones*, Oliver & Boyd, Edinburgh and London (1967)

Cooper, Lyn and Ray. *New Zealand Gemstones*, A.H. & A.W. Reed, Wellington, Auckland and Sydney (1969)

Delair, J. B. *Collecting Rocks and Fossils*, Batsford, London (1966)

Desautels, P. E. *The Mineral Kingdom*, Hamlyn, Feltham (1969)

Ellis, Clarence. *The Pebbles on the Beach*, Faber & Faber, London (1957)

Evans, I. O. *Rocks, Minerals and Gemstones*, Hamlyn, Feltham (1972)

Firsoff, V. A. *Gemstones of the British Isles*, Oliver & Boyd, Edinburgh and London (1971)

Fisher, P. J. *Jewels*, Batsford, London (1965)

Frondel, C. *The (Dana's) System of Mineralogy*, Wiley, New York (1962)

Greg, R. P. and Lettsom, W. G. *Manual of the Mineralogy of Great Britain and Ireland*, John van Voorst, London (1858)

Heddle, Forster M. *The Mineralogy of Scotland*, David Douglas, Edinburgh (1901)

Kirkcaldy, J. F. *Minerals and Rocks*, Blandford Press, London (1963)

Kraus, E. M. and Slawson, C. B. *Gems and Gem Materials*, McGraw-Hill, New York and London (1947)

Kunz, G. F. *Curious Lore of Precious Stones*, Constable, London (1972)

MacCallien, W. J. *Scottish Gemstones*, Quantum Reprints, London (1967)

McLintock, W. F. P. *A Guide to the Collection of Gemstones in the Geological Museum*, HMSO, London (1951)

Pearl, Richard M. *Introduction to the Mineral Kingdom*, Blandford Press, London (1966)

Perry, Ron and Nance. *Australian Gemstones*, A.H. & A.W. Reed, Wellington, Auckland and Sydney (1970)

Read, H. H. (ed). *Rutley's Elements of Mineralogy*, Murby, London (1970)

Rogers, Cedric. *A Collector's Guide to Minerals, Rocks and Gemstones in Cornwall and Devon*, Bradford Barton, Truro (1968)

Rogers, Cedric (ed) et al. *Finding Britain's Gems*, Lapidary Publications, London (1972)

Sinkansas, John. *Gemstones of North America*, Van Nostrand, New York (1972)

Sinkansas, John. *Standard Catalogue of Gems*, Van Nostrand, New York (1968)

Smith, H. G. F. *Gemstones*, Methuen, London (1952); revised edn Chapman and Hall, London (1973)

Spencer, L. J. *A Key to Precious Stones*, Blackie, Glasgow and London (1958)

Tennissen, A. C. *Colourful Mineral Identifier*, Sterling Publishing Co., New York (1969)

BIBLIOGRAPHY

Webster, Robert. *Gemmologist's Compendium*, N A G Press, London
  (1964)
Webster, Robert. *Practical Gemmology*, N A G Press, London (1966)
Webster, Robert. *Gems*, Butterworth, London (1970)
Weinstein, M. *Precious and Semi-precious Stones*, Pitman, London (1946)
Zim, H. S. and Shaffer, P. R. *Rocks and Minerals*, Hamlyn, London (1965)

PERIODICALS

Australian Lapidary Magazine, The, Bi-monthly, Jay Kay Publications,
  11 Robinson St, Sydney, New South Wales
Canadian Rockhound, Bi-monthly, PO Box 194, Station A, Vancouver,
  British Columbia
Gems, Monthly, Lapidary Publications, 29 Ludgate Hill, London EC4
Gems and Minerals, Monthly, PO Box 687, Mentone, California
Lapidary Journal, Monthly, 3564 Kettner Blvd, San Diego, California

INDEX